EXPLORING

AEGEAN

A Comprehensive Travel Guide to Greece's

Timeless Beauty

Stalwart Halves

TABLE OF CONTENT

CHAPTER 1

Introduction to the Aegean

The Aegean, a mesmerizing area located between the mainland of Greece and Turkey, is a place that generates a feeling of awe and takes guests to a world of timeless beauty. With its magnificent scenery, crystal-clear seas, interesting history, and active culture, the Aegean provides a genuinely immersive and fulfilling vacation experience.

Stretching over the eastern Mediterranean Sea, the Aegean is recognized for its collection of stunning islands, each holding its own particular appeal and attractiveness. From the world-famous Santorini with its distinctive blue-domed churches and awe-inspiring sunsets to the vibrant and cosmopolitan vibe of Mykonos, and the culturally rich and varied island of Crete, the Aegean islands constitute an archipelago of treasures waiting to be discovered.

Beyond the islands, the Aegean area is home to the historic city of Athens, the birthplace of democracy and a treasure trove of historical antiquities. Here, within the busy streets, is the beautiful Acropolis, towering above the city and showcasing the famed Parthenon.

As you roam around the old remains, you'll sense a strong connection to the beginning of Western civilisation.

One of the Aegean's most impressive qualities is its rich historical importance. The area served as the birthplace of ancient civilizations, seeing the rise and collapse of empires and the blossoming of famous cultures. Delphi, the temple of the Oracle, once attracted seekers of knowledge from far and wide, while Ephesus gives a look into the grandeur of both Greek and Roman civilizations. Knossos, the enormous palace complex of the Minoan civilisation, captivates with its elaborate architecture and fantastic legends.

While the Aegean possesses a rich historical tapestry, it is also a place of outstanding natural beauty. From the lovely beaches that cover the shoreline to the harsh terrain that comprise lush woods, towering cliffs, and ancient volcanoes, the Aegean's varied topography never ceases to astound. Adventurers may go on walks along picturesque paths, visit the awe-inspiring Samaria Gorge, or marvel at the volcanic marvels of Nisyros and the Santorini Caldera.

No tour around the Aegean would be complete without sampling its exquisite food. Greek cuisine, recognized internationally for its simplicity and freshness, is profoundly anchored in the Aegean's seaside tastes.

Indulge in luscious fish, drizzled with golden olive oil, and relish the pungent feta cheese that accompanies classic recipes. Food and wine festivals around the area give a chance to appreciate and sample the Aegean's gastronomic wonders.

The Aegean is not merely a location of physical beauty; it is also rich in mythology and traditions that have molded Western literature and culture. From the legendary abode of the gods, Mount Olympus, to the epic exploits documented in Homer's Odyssey, and the mythological islands that dot the Aegean Sea, this area is rich with stories of valor, romance, and divine intervention.

This comprehensive travel guide to the Aegean will take you on a voyage of discovery, including insights into the region's must-visit attractions, hidden jewels, cultural traditions, and practical recommendations for arranging your vacation. Whether you desire a relaxed beach holiday, a cultural immersion, an investigation of historical ruins, or an escape into nature's embrace, the Aegean promises to be an amazing place that will leave an everlasting stamp on your heart and soul.

The Aegean: A Window into Greece's Timeless Beauty

The Aegean Sea, a sparkling expanse of blue waves, embraces within its grasp a world of unsurpassed beauty and rich cultural legacy. Situated between the mainland of Greece and Turkey, the Aegean area provides an intriguing combination of history, mythology, breathtaking scenery, and warm Mediterranean hospitality. It is a spot where time appears to stand still, enabling guests to immerse themselves in Greece's eternal beauty.

The Aegean's captivating islands, spread like rare pearls over the water, are a key attraction of the area. These lovely isles catch the imagination with their white-washed settlements tumbling down slopes, tiny fishing coves, and stunning windmills. Each island has its own particular character, from the cosmopolitan appeal of Mykonos and the dramatic sunsets of Santorini to the unspoilt beauty of lesser-known jewels like Naxos or Paros. The Aegean islands tempt travelers to discover their secret coves, bathe in the warmth of the Mediterranean sun, and immerse themselves in the slow island way of life.

Beyond the islands, the Aegean's mainland is as attractive. The region's ancient capital, Athens, remains as a tribute to Greece's illustrious history. The city is a colorful combination of ancient marvels and contemporary refinement, where towering marble columns and ancient ruins mingle with bustling neighborhoods, stylish stores, and bright street art. As you wander through the small lanes of Plaka or stare upon the Acropolis sitting magnificently above the city, you can't help but feel a strong connection to the cradle of democracy and Western civilisation.

The Aegean's everlasting beauty is delicately intertwined into its ancient fabric. It is an area rich in mythology and stories that have impacted art, literature, and society for millennia. From the mythological birthplace of Zeus on the island of Crete to the legendary tales of Odysseus and the Sirens, the Aegean is a living incarnation of the ancient myths that continue to enchant the globe. Exploring the region's historic monuments, such as Delphi, Ephesus, and Knossos, enables guests to go back in time and immerse themselves in the intriguing history and mythology of Greece.

Nature has also been gracious to the Aegean, embellishing it with awe-inspiring vistas and natural treasures. The coastline is a patchwork of golden beaches, secret coves, and stunning cliffs that plummet into the sparkling water. The Aegean's hinterland includes beautiful valleys, craggy mountains, and rich plains, offering a paradise for nature aficionados and outdoor explorers. Whether you want to climb through stunning gorges, uncover secret waterfalls, or experience the volcanic wonders of Nisyros and the Santorini Caldera, the Aegean's natural splendor will leave you in amazement.

To genuinely comprehend the Aegean is to embrace its friendly and inviting culture. The region's inhabitants are noted for their genuine kindness, open hearts, and enthusiasm for sharing their traditions and customs. Delve into the colorful local festivals, where traditional music and dancing fill the air, and participate in the celebration of life, cuisine, and community. Engage with craftsmen conserving historic crafts, enjoy the flavors of the Aegean via its traditional food, and allow yourself to be wrapped in the warmth of Greek hospitality.

As a window into Greece's ageless beauty, the Aegean encourages guests to embark on a transforming trip. It is a location where ancient history and current life merge, where breathtaking landscapes provoke a feeling of awe, and where the fabled stories of gods and heroes come to life. Whether you are seeking leisure, adventure, cultural immersion, or just a chance to connect with the past, the Aegean provides an experience that is both engaging and memorable.

A Brief Overview of the Aegean Region

The Aegean region, located in the eastern Mediterranean Sea, is a mesmerizing location recognized for its spectacular natural beauty, lively culture, and rich historical past. Spanning over the shores of Greece and Turkey, this diversified area offers a plethora of islands, coastal towns, ancient monuments, and magnificent vistas.

The Aegean Sea itself is a stunning expanse of crystal-clear seas, noted by its deep blue colours and dispersed archipelagos. The sea works as a linking thread, bringing together the many aspects of the area and providing as a portal to its hidden riches. It has played a vital role throughout history, promoting commerce, cultural exchange, and marine exploration.

The Aegean islands, with their gorgeous scenery and charming ambience, are the crown jewels of the area. From the legendary Santorini, famed for its spectacular cliffs, whitewashed houses, and beautiful sunsets, to the cosmopolitan Mykonos, known for its active nightlife and premium resorts, the islands provide a broad variety of experiences for any tourist.

Other prominent islands are Rhodes, with its medieval old town and ancient ruins, Crete, the biggest and most diversified island in Greece, and Lesbos, noted for its gorgeous beaches and traditional towns.

The Aegean's mainland is as enthralling, with a variety of historical monuments and cultural attractions. Athens, the historic capital of Greece, is a lively city where ancient history perfectly merges with contemporary life. The

Acropolis, an iconic emblem of Western civilisation, rises majestically atop a rocky hill, containing the spectacular Parthenon and other historic monuments. Other important mainland locations include Thessaloniki, Greece's second-largest city, famed for its rich Byzantine legacy, and Ephesus in Turkey, a well-preserved ancient city that provides a look into the grandeur of the Roman Empire.

The Aegean area is a treasure trove for history aficionados. It was the origin of ancient Greek civilization, the heart of the Minoan and Mycenaean civilizations, and the scene for key historical events and wars. Ruins and archaeological sites are strewn across the area, enabling tourists to tread in the footsteps of past civilizations.

Delphi, home to the legendary Oracle of Apollo, gives a look into the magical realm of ancient Greek religion and prophesy. The remains of Troy, immortalized in Homer's Iliad, give a view into the famous Trojan War. These landmarks, along with numerous more, add to the region's historical importance and appeal.

The Aegean's natural beauty is equally appealing. The coastline is endowed with gorgeous beaches, quiet coves, and craggy cliffs, giving numerous chances for leisure and water-based sports like as swimming, snorkeling, and sailing.

The region's hinterland offers majestic mountain ranges, rich valleys, and lush woods, offering a paradise for nature lovers and adventure enthusiasts. From ascending the Samaria Gorge in Crete to seeing the volcanic landscapes of the Aegean islands, the region's natural beauties never fail to inspire awe.

The Aegean's culture is profoundly based in its historical history and Mediterranean way of life. The region's cuisine is a gourmet feast, comprising fresh fish, olive oil, fragrant herbs, and classic meals like as moussaka and souvlaki.

Festivals and festivities take place throughout the year, when people and tourists join together to delight in music, dancing, and cultural traditions. From traditional Greek music, known as rembetiko, to energetic folk dances like the syrtaki, the Aegean area provides a vivid and full cultural experience.

In essence, the Aegean area is a mesmerizing location that provides a wonderful combination of natural beauty, historical importance, and active culture. Whether you want to explore its picturesque islands, dig into its ancient history, or just rest on its pristine beaches, the Aegean guarantees an extraordinary experience that will leave you with a profound appreciation for its ageless attractiveness.

Practical Information for Exploring the Aegean

Exploring the Aegean is a fascinating journey that demands some practical measures to guarantee a smooth and pleasurable vacation. Whether you're intending to island-hop, visit historical monuments, or immerse yourself in the local culture, here are some practical suggestions and information to assist you traverse the Aegean region:

Visa and Entry Requirements: Before going to the Aegean, verify the visa requirements for Greece and Turkey, since they may differ based on your nationality. Ensure that your passport is valid for at least six months beyond your anticipated travel date.

Best Time to Visit: The Aegean area boasts a Mediterranean environment, typified by scorching summers and moderate winters. The main tourist season goes from June to August when the weather is bright and mild. However, if you prefer fewer people and nice weather, try coming during the shoulder seasons of spring (April-May) and fall (September-October).

Getting There: The primary international airports servicing the Aegean area are Athens International Airport (ATH) in

Greece and Istanbul Airport (IST) in Turkey. From there, you may connect to domestic aircraft or employ ferry services to reach your selected locations inside the Aegean.

Transportation: Island hopping is a popular method to visit the Aegean islands. Ferry services run between the main islands and offer a picturesque and delightful travel experience. It's essential to reserve your boat tickets in advance, particularly during high season. Additionally, domestic aircraft link major cities and islands in the area, giving a speedier option for greater distances.

Local Transportation: Once you've arrived at your destination, public transportation choices differ based on the locale. In major cities like Athens and Thessaloniki, you may depend on metro systems, buses, and taxis to get about. On the islands, local buses, rented vehicles, and scooters are major sources of mobility. Be cautious to verify the availability and regularity of public transit on each island, since it may vary.

Hotel: The Aegean provides a broad selection of hotel alternatives to meet diverse budgets and interests. From upscale resorts to boutique hotels, guesthouses, and vacation rentals, you'll find alternatives to match your requirements. Popular islands and tourist locations tend to provide a large selection of alternatives, but it's important to reserve in advance, particularly during high season.

Currency and Payments: Greece uses the Euro (€) as its currency, whereas Turkey uses the Turkish Lira (TRY). ATMs are generally accessible across the Aegean area, however it's a good idea to carry extra cash for little transactions and locations that may not take credit cards.

Credit cards are normally accepted at most businesses, however it's best to advise your bank of your trip intentions to prevent any payment difficulties.

Health and Safety: Ensure you have enough travel insurance that covers medical expenditures. It's also good to verify whether any immunizations are necessary before heading to the Aegean.

In terms of safety, the Aegean area is usually regarded secure for tourists, although it's always advisable to take conventional measures like securing your things and being mindful of your surroundings.

Local Customs and Etiquette: Familiarize oneself with the local customs and etiquette of the place. Greeks and Turks are recognized for their great hospitality, thus observing local customs and displaying civility will improve your interactions and experiences. Modest dress is often welcomed while visiting religious locations.

Language: Greek is the official language of Greece, whereas Turkish is spoken in Turkey. English is frequently spoken in tourist regions, but learning a few simple words in the local language may go a long way in developing relationships with the people.

By examining these practical advice and facts, you'll be well-prepared to explore the Aegean and make the most of your tour through Greece's ageless splendor. Enjoy your journey and absorb everything that this wonderful location has to offer!

CHAPTER 2

Island Hopping: Discovering Greece's Island Gems

Island hopping in Greece's Aegean Sea is a defining experience, enabling guests to see the country's numerous and stunning island treasures.

With over 6,000 islands and islets strewn around the Aegean, each with its own distinct character, history, and beauty, island hopping gives an opportunity to dig into the genuine spirit of Greece's coastal appeal. Here's a guide to help you go on a wonderful island-hopping adventure:

Plan Your Itinerary: Start by studying the islands that intrigue you the most. Consider variables such as their geographical closeness, ferry connections, and the experiences they provide.

Popular island clusters include the Cyclades, with classic destinations like Santorini and Mykonos, and the Dodecanese, with Rhodes and Kos. Other island groupings such as the Ionian Islands, Sporades, and Saronic Islands all have their particular attraction.

Choose Your Base: Select a beginning location or a base island from which you may begin your island-hopping quest. Athens is a frequent starting point, with Piraeus Port acting as the entryway to the Aegean. Alternatively, you might go for an island like Mykonos or Santorini, which have great ferry links and international airports.

Ferry Travel: Ferry services are the principal form of transit between the islands. Research boat timetables and book your tickets in advance, particularly during high season. High-speed ferries provide speedier connections but tend to be more costly.

Consider a combination of both high-speed and normal boats to maximize your journey time and costs.

Island features: Each island has its own allure and features. Santorini, noted for its magnificent sunsets and dramatic caldera vistas, is a must-visit for its famous white-washed structures and blue-domed churches.

Mykonos has a busy nightlife scene, gorgeous beaches, and lovely windmills. Crete, the biggest Greek island, features a rich history, lovely towns, and gorgeous beaches. Explore lesser-known islands like Naxos, Paros, or Milos for a more genuine and laid-back experience.

Duration of Stay: Plan your time on each island depending on your tastes and the island's size. Some islands may be visited completely in a day or two, while others may take longer time to truly appreciate their beauty. Strike a mix between famous places and off-the-beaten-path treasures to build a diversified itinerary.

Hidden Gems: Don't be afraid to travel off the main route and explore lesser-known islands. Explore islands like Amorgos, Folegandros, or Serifos, which provide a more calm and genuine experience. These hidden treasures frequently have isolated beaches, picturesque towns, and a slower pace of life, enabling you to immerse yourself in the genuine spirit of Greek island lifestyle.

Embrace Local Culture: Immerse yourself in the local culture of each island. Engage with the friendly inhabitants, enjoy traditional food at family-run tavernas, and join in local festivals and activities. Learn about the island's history, traditions, and rituals, which are frequently profoundly connected with the sea and environment.

Beach Exploration: Greece is famed for its magnificent beaches, and each island has its own set of coastline beauties. From the golden sandy beaches of Mykonos and the volcanic coasts of Santorini to the turquoise seas of Zakynthos and the secret coves of Milos, take time to relax, swim, and soak up the sun on these lovely coastlines.

Outdoor excursions: The islands provide opportunity for outdoor excursions. Hike along gorgeous paths, discover sea caves by kayak or boat, and embark on snorkeling or diving

trips to explore the abundant aquatic life. Take advantage of the natural settings and enjoy sports like windsurfing, sailing, or paddleboarding.

Record Memories: Finally, don't forget to record the amazing moments of your island-hopping voyage. From magnificent sunsets to picturesque alleys and renowned monuments, the Aegean islands provide many photo possibilities. Create lasting memories of your journey and share the beauty of Greece's island treasures with others.

Island hopping in the Aegean is a dream come true for many vacationers. With careful preparation, an adventurous attitude, and a desire to embrace the distinctive beauty of each island, you'll begin on a voyage that will leave you with amazing memories and a profound appreciation for Greece's island riches.

Choosing the Right Islands for Your Itinerary Subtitle

When organizing your island-hopping journey in the Aegean, picking the correct islands for your itinerary is vital to guarantee a well-rounded and rewarding experience. With countless islands to select from, each with its own individual charm, history, and attractions, here are some points to consider while choosing on the islands to include in your itinerary:

Island Groups: Familiarize yourself with the numerous island groups in the Aegean. The Cyclades, Ionian Islands, Dodecanese, Sporades, and Saronic Islands are among the most popular groupings. Each group has its own character, geography, and cultural influences. Research the islands within each category to locate the ones that fit with your interests and preferences.

Interests and Activities: Consider the sort of experiences you desire throughout your island-hopping adventure. Are you searching for bustling nightlife, stunning beaches, historical monuments, outdoor experiences, or a mix of these? Some islands, like Mykonos and Ios, are renowned for their bustling party scenes, while others, like as Crete and Naxos, provide a combination of beaches, historical ruins, and traditional towns. Identify the activities and attractions that appeal to you to limit down your selections.

Island Size and Accessibility: Take into consideration the size of the islands and their accessibility from your selected starting place. Larger islands like Crete and Rhodes provide a large selection of activities and facilities, making them suitable for extended vacations. Smaller islands like Paros and Milos give a more personal and relaxing vibe. Consider the ferry connections between islands to guarantee seamless transitions and reduce travel time.

Travel Season: The time of year you want to travel might impact your choice of islands. Popular islands like Santorini and Mykonos tend to be congested during peak season (June to August). If you want a calmer experience, try going during the shoulder seasons (April to May and September to October) when the weather is still great, and the crowds are lighter. Some islands, notably those in the Ionian group, have a longer tourist season and may provide additional possibilities outside the busy months.

Budget: Your budget might play a part in deciding the islands you visit. Some islands, particularly those renowned for luxury lodgings, upmarket cuisine, and cosmopolitan nightlife, might be more costly. However, Greece also provides budget-friendly choices, including inexpensive lodgings, small tavernas, and less touristic islands. Consider a combination of both to balance your budget while enjoying the richness of the Aegean.

Own tastes: Ultimately, your own tastes and travel style should drive your choice of islands. Reflect on what features of the Greek islands connect with you. Are you lured to the distinctive white-washed structures and beautiful sunsets of Santorini? Or do you like the real charm and slower pace of life on lesser-known islands? Consider the ambience, architecture, cultural legacy, and natural beauty that connect with you the most.

Flexibility: Keep an element of flexibility in your itinerary. While it's crucial to prepare ahead and obtain required reservations, make space for spontaneity. Leave some days unscheduled, so you may uncover hidden treasures or prolong your stay on an island that captivates you.

Remember, every island in the Aegean has its own distinct appeal, and there is no one-size-fits-all method to island hopping. By considering these elements and knowing your tastes, you can customise your schedule to create a memorable tour that displays the variety and beauty of the Greek islands.

Iconic Aegean Islands: Santorini, Mykonos, and Crete

The Aegean Sea is home to a number of magnificent islands, but three of the most famous and renowned destinations are Santorini, Mykonos, and Crete. Each of these islands provides a different experience, showing the beauty, charm, and cultural diversity of the Aegean area. Here's a deeper look at what makes these islands so special:

Santorini: Santorini is a dreamy island famed for its spectacular vistas, beautiful sunsets, and distinctive architecture. The island's characteristic white-washed houses with blue-domed roofs located on the cliffs of the caldera make a gorgeous and romantic environment. Must-see sights include the beautiful hamlet of Oia, noted for its sunset vistas, the ancient remains of Akrotiri, and the gorgeous Red Beach. Santorini also features great vineyards, where you may experience the island's peculiar volcanic wines. Don't miss the chance to indulge in wonderful local food and explore the island's bustling nightlife.

Mykonos: Mykonos is known with cosmopolitan elegance and boisterous party scenes. This bustling island draws travelers with its gorgeous sandy beaches, opulent resorts, and dynamic nightlife. The island's center, Mykonos Town, fascinates tourists with its quaint small alleys, famous windmills, and the famed waterfront neighborhood known as Little Venice. During the day, enjoy the sun and water at famous beaches including Paradise Beach and Super Paradise Beach. As night falls, Mykonos comes alive with its world-renowned clubs and bars, making it a favourite destination for visitors seeking a colorful and hedonistic environment.

Crete: As the biggest Greek island, Crete provides an immersive and varied experience. Rich in history, this island was the hub of the ancient Minoan culture, which you may discover at the archaeological site of Knossos. Crete also provides spectacular scenery, from gorgeous beaches to steep mountains and quaint towns. Visit the picturesque town of Chania with its Venetian port, explore the famed Samaria Gorge, or relax on the magnificent beaches of Elafonisi and Balos. Crete is also famed for its exquisite gastronomy, with traditional delicacies like dakos and fresh fish to eat.

These renowned islands provide a look into the eternal splendor of the Aegean area. Whether you desire romance, bustling nightlife, or a blend of history and natural grandeur, Santorini, Mykonos, and Crete deliver amazing experiences that appeal to varied interests and tastes. Embrace the distinct appeal of each island and make experiences that will last a lifetime.

Hidden Treasures: Lesser-known Aegean Islands

While Santorini, Mykonos, and Crete take the focus, the Aegean Sea is also home to lesser-known islands that possess their own particular attraction and provide a more private and off-the-beaten-path experience. These hidden jewels enable guests to experience a calmer side of the Aegean and immerse themselves in true Greek island culture. Here are some lesser-known Aegean islands that demand your attention:

Amorgos: Nestled in the southern Cyclades, Amorgos emits an unspoilt beauty and a tranquil ambience. This mountainous island is famed for its stunning cliffs, gorgeous beaches, and attractive settlements. Explore the renowned Monastery of Panagia Hozoviotissa, located on a cliffside, and enjoy stunning vistas. Hike through the island's picturesque paths, relax on isolated beaches like Agia Anna, and explore lovely villages like as Chora and Katapola.

Serifos: Serifos, part of the Western Cyclades, is a calm and pristine island that captivates travelers with its natural attractiveness. Its largest town, Chora, impresses with its historic white-washed homes and small lanes. Explore the historic iron mines and enjoy panoramic views from the hilltop castle. Swim on scenic beaches like Livadi and Psili Ammos, and taste fresh seafood in local tavernas.

Symi: Located near the Turkish coast, Symi is a lovely island famed for its colorful neoclassical houses and small port. The village of Gialos attracts travelers with its lovely waterfront, boutique shops, and seafood tavernas. Explore the island's rich nautical history at the Symi nautical Museum, and find secret coves like Nanou and Marathounda. A visit to the Panormitis Monastery, a spiritual center on the island, is highly advised.

Folegandros: Folegandros, part of the Cyclades, is a calm and untouched island with a relaxing attitude. Its largest town, Chora, built on a cliff, provides spectacular views of the Aegean Sea. Explore its twisting lanes, see the Panagia Church, and enjoy the sunset from the hilltop Panagia Square. Discover hidden beaches like Agali and Livadaki, and enjoy traditional hospitality in small tavernas.

Patmos: Known as the "Island of the Apocalypse," Patmos mixes natural beauty with spiritual importance. It is where St. John the Apostle composed the Book of Revelation. Visit the Monastery of Saint John, a UNESCO World Heritage Site, and visit the Cave of the Apocalypse. Wander around the lovely village of Chora, with its whitewashed buildings and small streets. Relax on gorgeous beaches like Psili Ammos and Agriolivado, and sample local cuisine at beachside tavernas.

Ikaria: Ikaria, situated in the eastern Aegean, is a laid-back island famed for its calm pace of life and longevity of its residents. Explore historic towns like Armenistis and Evdilos, and explore the hot springs of Therma for a revitalizing vacation. Discover stunning beaches like Seychelles and Nas, and immerse yourself on the island's rich cultural heritage, including its dynamic music and dance festivals.

These secret Aegean islands provide a calmer and more authentic experience, where you can escape the throng and connect with the real essence of Greece. From calm beaches and picturesque towns to historic landmarks and genuine hospitality, these hidden gems urge you to explore the lesser-known beauties of the Aegean.

The Aegean Sea is home to a number of magnificent islands, but three of the most famous and renowned destinations are Santorini, Mykonos, and Crete. Each of these islands provides a different experience, showing the beauty, charm, and cultural diversity of the Aegean area. Here's a deeper look at what makes these islands so special:

These renowned islands provide a look into the eternal splendor of the Aegean area. Whether you desire romance, bustling nightlife, or a blend of history and natural grandeur, Santorini, Mykonos, and Crete deliver amazing experiences that appeal to varied interests and tastes. Embrace the distinct appeal of each island and make experiences that will last a lifetime.

CHAPTER 3

Athens: The Gateway to the Aegean

As the capital city of Greece, Athens serves as the entrance to the Aegean area, linking tourists to the picturesque islands that dot the Aegean Sea. This ancient city not only has its own unique past but also gives simple transit alternatives to go on an exciting adventure around the Aegean. Here's why Athens should be a vital component of your Aegean exploration:

Historical and Cultural Significance: Athens is a rich mine of ancient history and culture, featuring renowned sites that illustrate the origin of Western civilisation. Explore the beautiful Acropolis, home to the Parthenon and other ancient buildings that have endured the test of time. Immerse yourself in the historical importance of monuments such as the Ancient Agora, the Temple of Olympian Zeus, and the Panathenaic Stadium. The city is also home to world-class institutions like the Acropolis Museum and the National Archaeological Museum, where you may dive deeper into Greece's ancient history.

Vibrant Urban Atmosphere: Athens is a busy city that harmoniously integrates antique and contemporary aspects. Stroll through the colorful areas of Plaka, Monastiraki, and Psiri, where historic buildings, small lanes, and attractive cafés provide an intriguing backdrop. Indulge in the city's lively street art culture, explore local markets like the Central Market (Varvakios Agora), and eat traditional Greek food in tavernas that line the streets.

Convenient Transportation center: As the transportation center of Greece, Athens has good links to the Aegean islands. The Port of Piraeus, situated only a short distance from the city center, acts as the primary ferry port, providing multiple daily departures to other islands. Whether you want to tour the Cyclades, Dodecanese, Ionian Islands, or any other island group, Athens offers a handy starting point for your island-hopping experience.

International Airport Access: Athens International Airport, Eleftherios Venizelos, links the city with key international destinations. This contemporary and well-connected airport provides flights from throughout the globe, making it simple to reach Athens and begin your Aegean tour. From the airport, you may easily reach the city core and continue your trip to the islands.

Pre- and Post-Island Exploration: Athens provides as a good base for pre- and post-island exploration. Before going on your island-hopping vacation, spend a few days in Athens to drink up its historical and cultural riches. After your island adventure, return to Athens and take advantage of its attractions, like as luxury hotels, exquisite cuisine, and exciting nightlife. Extend your stay to explore more of the city's hidden secrets and discover its modern art scene, bustling music venues, and stylish districts.

Unique City and Sea vistas: Athens provides breathtaking vistas that merge the metropolitan environment with the dazzling Aegean Sea. Ascend to heights like Lycabettus Hill or the Filopappou Hill for panoramic perspectives of the city and the Aegean shoreline. Witness spectacular sunsets over the metropolitan skyline and sight the faraway islands that await your exploration.

Athens is not merely a starting point; it is a destination in itself. It delivers a perfect combination of history, culture, and contemporary facilities, making it a vital aspect of any Aegean experience. Begin your adventure in Athens and let the city's vitality and legacy push you towards the timeless beauty of the Aegean islands.

Exploring the Historic City of Athens

Athens, the capital city of Greece, is a mesmerizing location rich in history and culture. From ancient ruins and archaeological sites to lively neighborhoods and busy marketplaces, Athens provides a unique combination of the old and the contemporary. Here's a guide to help you make the most of your tour of this ancient city:

Acropolis: Start your adventure with a visit to the Acropolis, the most recognizable monument in Athens. Towering above the city, the Acropolis is home to the Parthenon, a majestic temple dedicated to the goddess Athena. Explore the Propylaea, the Erechtheion, and the Temple of Athena Nike while enjoying panoramic views of the city from this historic stronghold.

Ancient Agora: Just a short walk from the Acropolis, you'll discover the Ancient Agora, the center of ancient Athens. This lively marketplace was a hub of political, commercial, and social activity. Explore the remains of the Stoa of Attalos, the Temple of Hephaestus, and the Agora Museum to gain a picture of everyday life in ancient Greece.

National Archaeological Museum: Immerse yourself in Greece's rich archaeological legacy by visiting the National Archaeological Museum. Housing a rich collection of objects from different eras of Greek history, the museum shows gems including the Mask of Agamemnon, the Antikythera Mechanism, and innumerable sculptures, ceramics, and jewelry.

Plaka: Wander around the lovely area of Plaka, situated at the foot of the Acropolis. With its tiny cobblestone lanes, neoclassical buildings, and small tavernas, Plaka gives a look into the old side of Athens. Explore the Anafiotika quarter, see the Museum of Greek Folk Art, and indulge in authentic Greek food at local eateries.

Monastiraki: Dive into the vivid ambiance of Monastiraki, a lively area noted for its busy flea market. Browse through a plethora of businesses providing antiques, handicrafts, and souvenirs. Visit the Monastiraki Square and the Tzistarakis Mosque, and enjoy some wonderful street cuisine from the local sellers.

Syntagma Square: Experience the heart of Athens in Syntagma Square, where you'll find the Hellenic Parliament and the famed Evzones, the ceremonial guards clothed in traditional garb.

Witness the changing of the guard ritual and take a walk around the National Gardens, a calm oasis in the center of the city.

Museums and Cultural Sites: Athens is a city of museums, giving a multitude of cultural experiences. Explore the Benaki Museum, devoted to Greek art and culture, or visit the Museum of Cycladic Art, showing the ancient Cycladic civilisation. Discover modern art at the Museum of modern Art and watch performances in the Odeon of Herodes Atticus, an old open air theater.

Mount Lycabettus: For panoramic views of Athens, climb or take a funicular up to Mount Lycabettus. At the summit, you'll be rewarded with stunning perspectives over the city, particularly after sunset. Enjoy a supper at the hilltop restaurant and marvel at the city lights as they flood the night sky.

Greek Cuisine: Athens is a heaven for food enthusiasts. Sample a vast assortment of Greek foods, from classic moussaka and souvlaki to fresh fish and delightful pastries. Explore the bustling Central Market (Varvakios Agora) to experience the sights, sounds, and tastes of local vegetables, spices, and meats.

Modern Athens: While Athens is famed for its historic attractions, it also embraces modernity. Discover modern art galleries,

fashionable bars, and rooftop restaurants with great views of the city. Explore the areas of Psiri and Gazi, noted for their active nightlife and cultural activities.

Athens is a city where the past and present coexist, enabling tourists to dig into the rich fabric of Greek history and immerse themselves in the vivid energy of a contemporary metropolis.

With its historical treasures, colorful districts, and gastronomic pleasures, Athens provides an amazing trip through time and culture.

Acropolis and Parthenon: A Journey into Ancient Greece

The Acropolis and the Parthenon remain as outstanding testaments to the grandeur and architectural prowess of ancient Greece. Perched high above the city of Athens, they have survived the test of time, enthralling tourists with their beauty and historical importance. Embark on a trip into ancient Greece as you tour the Acropolis and marvel at the Parthenon.

The Acropolis: The Acropolis, meaning "high city," is a fortified hilltop castle that dominates the Athens skyline. As you scale the hill, you'll be transported back in time to the golden period of Athens. This UNESCO World Heritage Site was the hub of the ancient city and served as a symbol of its cultural and political dominance. Walk through the magnificent Propylaea, the doorway to the holy sanctuary, and see its stunning marble columns.

Witness the Temple of Athena Nike, a magnificent temple devoted to the goddess of victory. Explore the Erechtheion, an ornate temple with its famed Porch of the Caryatids, containing sculptures of maidens. Finally, reach the peak of the Acropolis and witness the gorgeous Parthenon.

The Parthenon: The Parthenon, an architectural marvel, sits as the crowning gem of the Acropolis. Built in the 5th century BC, this Doric temple was devoted to the city's patron goddess, Athena Parthenos. Marvel at its majestic marble columns and the beautifully carved metopes and friezes that cover its façade.

Despite centuries of wear and deterioration, the Parthenon continues to inspire awe with its harmonious proportions and beautiful workmanship. Enter the temple and picture the ancient rites and ceremonies that previously took place inside its holy walls.

Historical value: The Acropolis and the Parthenon retain tremendous historical value. They represent the cradle of democracy and the apex of Athenian accomplishments in art, architecture, and philosophy. The Parthenon itself is a testimony to the cultural and intellectual advances of ancient Greece.

It functioned as a treasury, a place of worship, and a symbol of Athenian pride. Through the ages, the Acropolis underwent significant modifications, including Byzantine, Frankish, and Ottoman occupations. It underwent repair attempts to maintain its architectural magnificence and cultural heritage.

Acropolis Museum: Enhance your voyage into ancient Greece by visiting the Acropolis Museum, situated at the southeastern slope of the Acropolis. This contemporary museum shows a unique collection of ancient relics uncovered at the Acropolis site.

Admire the stunning marble sculptures, elaborate friezes, and architectural remnants that reveal insights into the history and craftsmanship of ancient Athens. The museum's top-floor Parthenon Gallery gives a rare chance to examine the surviving Parthenon sculptures, known as the Elgin Marbles, in a beautiful setting built to imitate their original arrangement.

Panoramic vistas: Besides its historical value, the Acropolis provides stunning panoramic vistas of Athens. As you stand atop the hill, gaze at the metropolis stretched out before you, with the wide metropolitan environment mixing with ancient ruins. Take in the panoramas of Mount Lycabettus, the Aegean Sea in the distance, and the new communities that have risen around the old city.

The Acropolis and the Parthenon are not merely architectural marvels; they are gates to ancient Greece, affording a look into the incredible accomplishments and cultural heritage of this magnificent civilisation. Explore these majestic monuments, immerse yourself in their historical importance, and let the grandeur of the Acropolis and the Parthenon transport you to a bygone period of myth and glory.

Beyond the Acropolis: Uncovering Athens' Modern Charms

While the Acropolis and its magnificent Parthenon justifiably capture the focus in Athens, this bustling city has much more to offer beyond its historical treasures. Athens is a dynamic city that perfectly mixes history with contemporary flare, giving a myriad of modern delights to discover.

Here are some highlights that will take you beyond the Acropolis and immerse you in the lively soul of Athens:

Neighborhoods with Character: Discover the different and colorful areas that give Athens its particular appeal. Start with Kolonaki, an affluent neighbourhood famed for its boutique boutiques, art galleries, and exquisite cafés.

Explore the bohemian area of Exarcheia, home to street art, alternative culture, and a thriving nightlife scene. Visit the fashionable district of Psiri, filled with hip clubs, elegant eateries, and live music venues. Each district has its own particular character and gives an insight into the present pulse of Athens.

Contemporary Art Scene: Athens has evolved as a hotspot for contemporary art, with various galleries and art venues showing the works of local and international artists. Visit the National Museum of Contemporary Art, situated in the old Fix brewery, and explore its collection of contemporary artworks.

Explore the vibrant art neighborhood of Metaxourgeio, where old industrial premises have been turned into art galleries and cultural organizations. Keep a look out for street art, as Athens is home to an incredible collection of murals and graffiti that provide a colorful and dynamic touch to the city's streets.

Gourmet Delights: Indulge your taste buds at Athens' booming gastronomic industry. From classic tavernas providing exquisite Greek food to modern eateries offering a blend of tastes, Athens offers something to please every pallet.

Visit the primary food market, Varvakios Agora, to enjoy the vivid sights, sounds, and fragrances of local vegetables and delicacies. Explore the areas of Koukaki and Gazi, where you'll discover a broad choice of eating options, from classic Greek tavernas to trendy cafés providing worldwide cuisines.

Rooftop Bars and vistas: Experience Athens from a fresh viewpoint by visiting its rooftop bars and enjoying spectacular panoramic vistas. Watch the sunset while drinking drinks at one of the rooftop bars in Monastiraki or Plaka, affording stunning perspectives of the Acropolis. Alternatively, travel to the contemporary area of Gazi, where you'll discover fashionable rooftop venues with a dynamic atmosphere and amazing metropolitan views.

Shopping Extravaganza: Athens is a shopper's dream, featuring a mix of high end shops, designer stores, and local markets. Stroll along Ermou Street, the city's major shopping boulevard, packed with worldwide brands and department shops. For a more distinctive shopping experience, browse the trendy boutiques and independent stores in the areas of Kolonaki and Koukaki. Don't miss the Sunday flea market in Monastiraki, where you can seek for vintage clothes, antiques, and unusual souvenirs.

Parks & Green Spaces: Take a break from the urban rush and bustle and escape to Athens' green oasis. The National Gardens, situated near Syntagma Square, provides a calm respite with its lush foliage, shaded walks, and tiny lakes. Visit the Stavros Niarchos Foundation Cultural Center, a contemporary architectural masterpiece including a park, a library, and the Greek National Opera. Enjoy a leisurely stroll down the promenade of Flisvos Marina, dotted with cafés, restaurants, and gorgeous boats.

Athens is a city of contrasts, where antique beauties combine perfectly with contemporary pleasures. By traveling beyond the Acropolis, you'll encounter the city's modern attractions, colorful communities, art scene, gastronomic pleasures, and much more.

Embrace the vitality and inventiveness that distinguish contemporary Athens, and let the city's modern attractiveness compliment your trip through its timeless past.

CHAPTER 4

Delving into History: Ancient Sites of the Aegean

The Aegean area of Greece is a treasure mine of ancient history and archaeological splendor. From majestic temples to ancient towns, experiencing the historic monuments of the Aegean is like going back in time.

Embark on a voyage through the annals of civilisation as you dig into the rich historical fabric of this enchanting location. Here are some of the fascinating ancient places that await your discovery:

Delos: Situated in the Cyclades archipelago, Delos is one of the most significant ancient sites in Greece. Considered a holy island in Greek mythology and the birthplace of Apollo and Artemis, Delos contains well-preserved remains that allow an insight into the island's previous splendour.

Explore the Terrace of the Lions, the House of Dionysus, the Temple of Isis, and the old theater as you travel around this UNESCO World Heritage site.

Knossos: Located on the island of Crete, Knossos is an ancient Minoan metropolis that goes back to the Bronze Age. The remains of Knossos give insights into the complex society that existed here circa 2000 BC.

Marvel at the Palace of Knossos, a huge edifice filled with brilliant murals, beautiful mosaics, and tortuous passages. Learn about the stories and traditions related with the Minotaur and the labyrinth, as you tour the ancient city's archaeological treasures.

Ephesus: Although not situated in Greece, the ancient city of Ephesus in Turkey is readily accessible from the Aegean area and is a must-visit for history aficionados. Ephesus was a thriving Roman city and a significant center of commerce and culture.

Explore the well-preserved remains of the Library of Celsus, the Great Theater, the Temple of Artemis, and the Terrace Houses, which provide an insight into the lifestyle of the city's rich citizens.

Ancient Olympia: Journey to the Peloponnese area to explore Ancient Olympia, the origin of the Olympic Games. Walk in the footsteps of historic athletes as you visit the archaeological site that previously held the famed sporting championships. Admire the Temple of Zeus, the old stadium, the gymnasium, and the Philippeion, a circular monument erected to Philip II of Macedon.

Mycenae: Venture into the mythological land of Mycenae, an ancient city that was once the hub of the great Mycenaean civilisation.

Marvel at the majestic Lion Gate, the gateway to the old city, and explore the remnants of the royal complex. Discover the Treasury of Atreus, a magnificent beehive-shaped tomb, and breathe in the ambiance of this UNESCO World Heritage site that inspired ancient Greek stories.

Ancient Thira: Perched on a cliff on the island of Santorini, Ancient Thira gives a look into the island's ancient history. Climb the steep hill to examine the relics of this ancient city, which dates back to the 9th century BC. Discover the remnants of buildings, temples, and old pathways, and enjoy panoramic views of the Aegean Sea and the volcanic environment of Santorini.

Akrotiri: Also situated on Santorini, Akrotiri is a remarkable archaeological site that exhibits the vestiges of an old Minoan village buried beneath volcanic ash. Often referred to as the "Pompeii of the Aegean," Akrotiri gives a rare view into the everyday life and complex civilisation that existed here before the volcanic catastrophe. Explore the well-preserved structures, beautiful frescoes, and relics that give significant insights into the Bronze Age Aegean.

Samothrace: Visit the island of Samoth race in the northern Aegean Sea to discover the ancient Sanctuary of the Great Gods. This holy location was known in ancient times and drew visitors from all across the Greek world.

Marvel at the enigmatic Winged Victory of Samothrace, a beautiful monument that now lies in the Louvre Museum in Paris, and find the vestiges of the temple complex and the old theater.

Pergamon: Located in modern-day Turkey but historically tied to the Aegean area, Pergamon was an ancient Greek city and an important cultural and political center.

Explore the remnants of the acropolis, including the magnificent Library of Pergamon and the Theater of Pergamon, which could seat up to 10,000 people. Marvel at the Altar of Zeus, an amazing building that once stood as one of the Seven Wonders of the Ancient World.

Assos: Nestled on the Aegean coast of Turkey, Assos is a gorgeous old city with a rich history. Wander among the remnants of the old community, including the Temple of Athena, the agora, and the spectacular city walls.

Enjoy the spectacular views of the Aegean Sea and the surrounding island of Lesbos from this lovely setting.

These historic monuments of the Aegean area give a riveting peek into the past, enabling you to connect with the civilizations that once flourished in this wonderful corner of the globe.

Immerse yourself in the tales, traditions, and architectural wonders as you explore the mysteries of these ancient civilizations and increase your understanding for the rich cultural legacy of the Aegean.

Ancient Ruins of Delphi: The Oracle's Sanctuary

Nestled among the craggy slopes of Mount Parnassus, the ancient ruins of Delphi have a particular position in Greek mythology and history. Revered as the center of the universe by the ancient Greeks, Delphi was home to the famed Oracle of Delphi, where seekers of knowledge sought heavenly direction.

Today, the archaeological site of Delphi allows tourists a chance to explore the relics of this hallowed sanctuary and immerse themselves in the mysterious air of the Oracle. Here's a glance at the ancient ruins of Delphi:

The Oracle of Delphi: Delphi was considered to be the residence site of Apollo, the god of prophecy, and his oracle acted as a conduit for divine communication. Pilgrims from far and wide traveled to Delphi to visit the Oracle, seeking answers to their burning concerns and direction for vital choices.

Delve into the history and importance of the Oracle as you tour the Temple of Apollo, where the priestess Pythia gave her mysterious forecasts.

The holy Way: Embark on a trek through the Sacred Way, the ancient road that took visitors through a succession of holy sites and constructions. This walkway, flanked with riches and sculptures, signified the pilgrims' spiritual climb towards the Oracle.

Wonder at the restored Treasury of the Athenians, the exquisite Stoa of the Athenians, and the spectacular Polygonal Wall, an architectural wonder that offered stability to the holy place.

The theatrical: The Theater of Delphi, built on the hillside above the sanctuary, is a superb example of ancient Greek theatrical design. Take a seat in this well-preserved amphitheater and imagine the echoes of ancient performances that once rang inside its stone walls.

Enjoy panoramic views of the surrounding environment, including the olive trees and the sweeping panoramas of the Gulf of Corinth.

The Stadium: Venture farther up the slope to uncover the ancient Stadium of Delphi, where athletic competitions and the Pythian Games were staged. Step onto the track and visualize the furious rivalry that transpired in this historic athletic stadium. From here, enjoy beautiful views of the sanctuary and the valley below.

Delphi Museum: Enhance your visit to the ancient remains by touring the Delphi Museum, situated near the archaeological site. The museum exhibits an amazing collection of items unearthed at Delphi, including sculptures, friezes, and votive offerings. Admire the renowned Charioteer of Delphi, a masterwork of ancient bronze sculpture, and dive into the complexities of ancient Greek art and workmanship.

Delphi Landscape: The natural environment of Delphi is as awe-inspiring as its ancient ruins. As you visit the site, marvel at the beautiful vistas of the surrounding countryside, typified by the rocky mountains, grassy valleys, and the shimmering waters of the Gulf of Corinth. Take a minute to absorb in the tranquil ambiance and connect with the magical energy that has attracted people to this hallowed location for generations.

The ancient remains of Delphi provide a compelling trip into the mythical and historical fabric of ancient Greece. As you travel along the footsteps of pilgrims and seekers of knowledge, you'll be transported to a period when Delphi had immense religious and cultural importance. Immerse yourself in the mystical air of the Oracle's refuge and let the whispers of the past guide your investigation of this unique archaeological site.

Ephesus: A Glimpse into Ancient Greek and Roman

Ephesus, situated in present-day Turkey, is a spectacular archaeological site that gives a fascinating glimpse into the rich history of both ancient Greek and Roman civilizations.

Once a renowned city of the Roman Empire, Ephesus prospered as a busy commerce and cultural hub. Today, its well-preserved remains give a compelling view into the everyday life, architecture, and majesty of this ancient metropolis. Let's go on a trip through time as we discover the intriguing legacy of Ephesus:

The Great Theater: Begin your journey with a visit to the Great Theater, a spectacular amphitheater that formerly held up to 25,000 people. Marvel at the grandeur of its architectural architecture and picture the lively acts that once adorned its stage. This landmark edifice serves as a tribute to the remarkable technical and aesthetic accomplishments of the ancient world.

The Library of Celsus: One of the most spectacular buildings in Ephesus is the Library of Celsus. Admire its perfectly repaired front, embellished with delicate sculptures and figures. This library formerly contained thousands of scrolls and served as a symbol of wisdom and scholarship. Standing before its majestic exterior, one can almost sense the intellectual and cultural vibrancy that filled the streets of ancient Ephesus.

The Temple of Artemis: Although hardly much remains of the Temple of Artemis, one of the Seven Wonders of the Ancient World, its historical value cannot be disregarded. This holy sanctuary was devoted to the Greek goddess Artemis and functioned as a focal point for religious devotion and cultural activities. Explore the ruins and envision the beauty that once encircled this great temple.

The Terrace Houses: Step into the life of the wealthier citizens of Ephesus by visiting the Terrace Houses. These exquisite mansions, filled with superbly preserved paintings and delicate mosaics, provide an insight into the richness and luxury experienced by the city's aristocracy. Wander around the well-preserved apartments, courtyards, and passageways, and get insight into the household life and social organization of ancient Ephesus.

The Agora: At the core of each ancient city was the Agora, a lively marketplace and social centre. In Ephesus, the Agora functioned as the hub of economic, political, and social activity.

Explore the remains of this lively marketplace, envisioning the merchants, craftsmen, and inhabitants that once filled its streets. Marvel at the massive columns and buildings that once decorated this flourishing public area.

The Roman Baths: Experience the splendor of ancient Roman life by visiting the Roman Baths of Ephesus. These enormous bathing facilities were not only locations for bodily cleaning but also functioned as social and recreational meeting sites. As you wander through the well-preserved remains, picture the opulent settings, intricate decorations, and lively atmosphere that once defined these magnificent bathing facilities.

The Odeon: Discover the Odeon, a tiny theater-like building that housed musical performances, recitations, and philosophical discussions. Admire the well-preserved chairs and envision the intellectual and cultural conversation that took place inside these walls. The Odeon serves as a tribute to the aesthetic and intellectual accomplishments of ancient Ephesus.

Ephesus gives a rare chance to experience the blending of Greek and Roman cultures. From its huge theaters and colossal libraries to its busy markets and elegant houses, the remains of Ephesus give a vivid look into the everyday life, cultural accomplishments, and architectural wonders of ancient times. Embark on this enthralling voyage and let the echoes of the past take you to a realm of classical magnificence and historical relevance.

Knossos: Minoan Civilization's Majestic Palace

Deep beneath the island of Crete sits the ancient city of Knossos, an archaeological site that displays the majesty and brilliance of the Minoan culture. Knossos was once the seat of Minoan power and culture, and its majestic palace remains as a witness to the sophisticated architectural and artistic accomplishments of this ancient civilisation. Let's explore into the interesting history and extraordinary aspects of Knossos:

Mythology and Discovery: According to Greek mythology, Knossos was the mythological abode of King Minos, who presided over a labyrinth that harbored the terrible Minotaur. The site of Knossos was unearthed in the late 19th century by the British archaeologist Sir Arthur Evans. Excavations found a large palace complex that gave vital insights into the Minoan civilisation.

The Palace Complex: The palace of Knossos was an architectural masterpiece, including many structures, courtyards, and convoluted passageways. Explore the well-preserved remains and observe the complex elements of the palace's construction. Marvel at the majestic stairs, columned halls, and colorful paintings that covered the palace walls. The arrangement of the palace reveals a hierarchical social structure and a profound grasp of urban planning.

The Throne Room: One of the most spectacular rooms inside the palace is the Throne Room, thought to be the ceremonial center of Knossos. The area has a massive gypsum throne covered with bright murals portraying religious and mythical subjects. Stand in wonder at the complex designs and brilliant hues that have endured the test of time.

The magnificent Staircase: Ascend the magnificent staircase of the palace and picture the dignitaries and nobility who once ascended these stairs. The stairway is covered with paintings representing images of processions, everyday life, and religious rites. These artworks give significant views into the Minoan civilization and their creative skill.

The Central Court: The central court of Knossos functioned as a centre for many activities. Its open space was encircled by colonnades and buildings that presumably contained administrative offices, workshops, and residential spaces. Imagine the colorful atmosphere of this busy courtyard, where people met for social and cultural activities.

The Hall of the Double Axes: Another famous room inside the palace is the Hall of the Double Axes. This chamber displays a distinctive emblem, the double axe, which was an important theme in Minoan religious and cultural traditions. Explore the beautifully adorned walls and attempt to comprehend the meaning behind the exquisite paintings.

The Queen's Megaron: Discover the Queen's Megaron, thought to be the residential quarters of an important female figure in Minoan culture. Admire the magnificent architecture, particularly the well-preserved baths and the elaborate paintings that represent images of nature and religious activities. The Queen's Megaron gives insights into the sophisticated lifestyle and aesthetic interests of the Minoan aristocracy.

Visiting Knossos enables you to immerse yourself in the intriguing world of the Minoan culture. Explore the enormous palace complex, stand in wonder of the beautiful artwork, and envisage the colorful life that once existed inside its walls. Knossos is a witness to the Minoans' excellent building methods, sophisticated culture, and their enduring effect on the history of ancient civilizations.

CHAPTER 5

Coastal Marvels: Beaches and Coastal Towns

The Aegean area is famed for its gorgeous coastline, filled with stunning beaches and attractive coastal villages. Whether you seek tranquility on pure sandy coastlines or prefer the colorful ambiance of seaside villages, the Aegean provides a multitude of coastal beauties to meet any traveler's need. Here are some of the stunning beaches and coastal villages you may explore:

Mykonos: This legendary Greek island is known with luxury, bustling nightlife, and gorgeous beaches. From the iconic Paradise Beach and Super Paradise Beach, known for their busy beach clubs and parties, to the tranquil Psarou Beach and Agios Ioannis Beach, Mykonos offers a broad variety of coastal experiences. Explore the lovely alleyways of Mykonos Town, where classic whitewashed houses and vibrant bougainvillea make a stunning background.

Santorini: Known for its breathtaking cliffside towns and beautiful sunsets, Santorini features distinctive coastline beauty. Visit the red and black volcanic sand beaches of Perissa and Kamari, where you may relax and soak up the sun. Explore the picturesque village of Oia, nestled on the caldera cliffs, and enjoy stunning views of the Aegean Sea. Don't miss the chance to take a boat journey to the adjacent volcanic islands and bathe in the hot springs.

Paros: Paros provides a combination of laid-back beach moods and classic Greek island charm. The beautiful sandy beaches of beautiful Beach and Santa Maria Beach are popular among water sports enthusiasts, while the hidden coves of Kolymbithres provide a calm respite.

Explore the gorgeous seaside villages of Naoussa and Parikia, where you can meander through small alleys, appreciate the Cycladic architecture, and eat wonderful seafood at waterfront tavernas.

Rhodes: With its rich history and magnificent shoreline, Rhodes is an intriguing location. The vast sandy beaches of Faliraki and Tsambika are great for sunbathing and water sports, while the quaint town of Lindos provides a pleasant seaside experience. Explore the old Old Town of Rhodes, a UNESCO World Heritage site, and promenade along the ancient walls with panoramic views of the sea.

Chios: Known for its pristine beauty and traditional charm, Chios is a hidden treasure in the Aegean. The pebble beaches of Mavra Volia and Karfas provide a tranquil location to unwind and enjoy crystal-clear seas. Explore the historic hamlet of Mesta, with its tiny lanes and stone cottages, or visit the famed Mastiha villages and learn about the island's distinctive Mastiha farming.

Naxos: Naxos features some of the most magnificent beaches in the Aegean. Plaka Beach and Agia Anna Beach provide lengthy expanses of golden sand and blue seas, excellent for sun-seekers and water sports aficionados. Visit the lovely seaside village of Naxos village, with its Venetian castle and busy waterfront promenade dotted with restaurants and cafés.

Thassos: Situated in the northern Aegean, Thassos provides a blend of lush green scenery and blue waves. Golden Beach, also known as Chrisi Ammoudia, is a magnificent sandy beach that draws tourists with its crystal-clear waters and attractive surroundings. Explore the seaside village of Limenas, with its historic sites and gorgeous port.

These are just a few examples of the seaside treasures awaiting you in the Aegean area. Whether you desire leisure, bustling nightlife, or a look into the traditional Greek island culture, the beaches and coastal towns of the Aegean provide a choice of activities to create memorable memories. Dive into the blue seas, soak in the sun, and appreciate the wonderful coastline beauty that makes the Aegean a veritable heaven for beach lovers.

Sun-Kissed Splendor: Aegean's Best Beaches

The Aegean area is endowed with an abundance of magnificent beaches that display the sun-kissed magnificence of this coastal paradise. From silky golden sands to crystal-clear turquoise seas, these beaches provide a great vacation for sun-seekers, water enthusiasts, and nature lovers alike. Here are some of the Aegean's top beaches that will leave you in awe of their natural beauty:

Navagio Beach, Zakynthos: Also known as Shipwreck Beach, Navagio Beach is one of the most renowned beaches in the Aegean. Enclosed by towering limestone cliffs and accessible only by boat, this isolated paradise has pristine white beaches and brilliant blue seas. The centerpiece of the beach is the wrecked ship that lays on its sand, providing a postcard-perfect image.

Elafonisi Beach, Crete: Located on the southwestern coast of Crete, Elafonisi Beach is a magnificent combination of pink sand, crystal-clear waves, and a lagoon filled with little islands. The shallow waves make it great for families, and the unusual pink tints of the sand, caused by shattered seashells, add to its attractiveness.

Balos Beach, Crete: Situated on the northwestern coast of Crete, Balos Beach is a real natural beauty. Accessible by boat or a beautiful stroll, this beach has a lovely lagoon with turquoise seas and a crescent-shaped expanse of fine white sand. The neighboring craggy cliffs and the little island of Gramvousa further enhance its charm.

Super Paradise Beach, Mykonos: Known for its dynamic beach club scene and boisterous environment, Super Paradise Beach in Mykonos is a sanctuary for partygoers and beach lovers. The golden beaches, sparkling seas, and a background of craggy cliffs make an alluring scene for sunbathing, swimming, and enjoying beachfront parties.

Sarakiniko Beach, Milos: Unlike any other beach in the Aegean, Sarakiniko Beach in Milos resembles a moonscape with its bizarre white volcanic rock formations. The contrast between the pristine white rocks and the deep blue seas is fascinating, making it a favorite among photographers and those seeking a distinctive beach experience.

Red Beach, Santorini: Located near the ancient settlement of Akrotiri, Red Beach is noted for its striking red volcanic cliffs and the contrasting deep blue seas. While the beach itself is modest, the spectacular backdrop and unusual geological formations make it a must-visit site for nature aficionados.

Koukounaries Beach, Skiathos: Nestled on the island of Skiathos, Koukounaries Beach is famed for its beautiful golden sand and crystal-clear waves. Surrounded by a deep pine forest, this beach provides a calm respite and is a dream for sunbathers, swimmers, and water sports lovers.

Psili Ammos Beach, Samos: Tucked away on the island of Samos, Psili Ammos Beach fascinates travelers with its pristine natural beauty. With its excellent sand, green seas, and tranquil ambiance, it gives a serene getaway away from the masses.

Plaka Beach, Naxos: Plaka Beach on the island of Naxos provides a lengthy stretch of smooth sand and gorgeous blue waves. With its modest depth and moderate waves, it is great for families and people seeking a calm beach experience.

St. Paul's Bay, Rhodes: Situated near the historic village of Lindos, St. Paul's Bay is a lovely cove with crystal-clear seas and a little sandy beach. Enclosed by steep cliffs, it emits a serene and solitary ambience, excellent for couples and those searching for a romantic break.

These are just a handful of the sun-kissed splendors that greet you in the Aegean. Each beach provides a distinct experience, combining natural beauty, clear seas, and the warm embrace of the Mediterranean sun.

Whether you prefer adventure, leisure, or a dynamic beach scene, the Aegean's top beaches are guaranteed to leave you with vivid memories of your coastal excursions.

Charming Coastal Towns: Nafplio, Chania, and Bodrum

Beyond the gorgeous beaches of the Aegean, lovely coastal towns appeal with their ancient charm, scenic scenery, and dynamic culture. These communities give an insight into the region's rich history and provide a chance to immerse oneself in the local way of life. Let's discover three of the most stunning seaside towns in the Aegean: Nafplio, Chania, and Bodrum.

Nafplio, Greece: Nestled on the eastern coast of the Peloponnese, Nafplio is a charming village that mixes Venetian, Ottoman, and Greek architectural influences. As Greece's first capital after independence, Nafplio emits a feeling of grandeur and historic importance. Stroll down the small cobblestone alleys of the old town, known as "Palia Poli," and marvel at the well-preserved neoclassical buildings, lovely squares, and flower-filled balconies.

Don't miss the renowned Palamidi Fortress, built on a hill overlooking the town and affording panoramic views of the Argolic Gulf. The Bourtzi Fortress, located on a tiny island in the bay, adds to the town's charm. With its busy seaside promenade dotted with cafés, tavernas, and boutique stores,

Nafplio captivates travelers with its romantic environment and cultural riches.

Chania, Greece: Located on the northwest coast of Crete, Chania is a compelling combination of Venetian, Ottoman, and Greek influences. The Old Town, with its small labyrinthine alleyways and colorful Venetian and Ottoman buildings, takes travelers back in time.

Explore the scenic Venetian Harbor, where ancient structures, like the majestic Firkas Fortress and the renowned lighthouse, form a postcard-perfect environment. Wander around the busy market, where the fragrances of native spices and the vivid variety of fresh food fill the air.

Chania's bustling waterfront promenade, surrounded with waterfront cafés and restaurants, encourages tourists to experience Cretan cuisine and enjoy breathtaking views of the Mediterranean Sea. With its rich history, engaging culture, and spectacular beauty, Chania enchants tourists from over the globe.

Bodrum, Turkey: Situated on the southwestern coast of Turkey, Bodrum is a wonderful beach town that flawlessly integrates history, culture, and natural beauty. Bodrum's historic heritage is visible in the towering Bodrum Castle, also known as the Castle of St. Peter, which overlooks the port. Explore the small alleyways of the old town, with its whitewashed cottages covered with vivid bougainvillea, boutique stores, and delightful cafés. Visit the old theater, dating back to the 4th century BCE, and envision the acts that previously enchanted crowds.

Bodrum's active harbor is a hive of activity, providing a wealth of culinary choices, energetic nightlife, and chances for boating and yacht trips.

The town's stunning beaches, including as Gumbet and Bitez, attract tourists to rest on golden dunes and swim in blue seas. Bodrum's unique combination of history, beach appeal, and energetic atmosphere make it a must-visit destination in the Aegean.

These lovely seaside cities of Nafplio, Chania, and Bodrum provide a fascinating combination of history, culture, and natural beauty. Immerse yourself in their distinct atmospheres, see their ancient monuments, sample the local food, and embrace the wonderful hospitality of the Aegean shore.

Sailing the Aegean: Exploring the Coast by Boat

One of the most fascinating ways to enjoy the Aegean is by sailing its blue seas and exploring the magnificent shoreline at your own speed. Sailing enables you to find secret coves, lonely islands, and private beaches that are typically unreachable by land. Whether you're a seasoned sailor or a first-time explorer, setting sail in the Aegean provides a unique and fascinating experience. Here's a look of the delights of sailing the Aegean and seeing its lovely shoreline by boat:

Opportunity to discover: Sailing allows you the opportunity to set your own path and discover the Aegean's coastline beauties at your leisure. With innumerable islands and hidden jewels along the coast, you may anchor in peaceful coves, find pristine beaches, and visit lovely fishing communities that are off the main road. The feeling of freedom and adventure that sailing gives is unequaled.

Crystal-clear Waters: The Aegean Sea is famed for its crystal-clear waters, making it a paradise for snorkelers and divers. While sailing, you may dock amid vivid coral reefs, underwater caverns, and historic shipwrecks, immersing yourself in the spectacular underwater environment. Dive into the blue depths, swim with colorful fish, and wonder at the aquatic life that flourishes under the surface.

Island Hopping: Sailing enables you to partake in the popular Greek pastime of island hopping. With over 200 inhabited islands in the Aegean, each with its own distinct character and charm, the alternatives are unlimited.

From the famed Cyclades, including Mykonos and Santorini, to the lesser-known treasures like the Dodecanese islands and the Sporades, you may construct your own schedule and cruise from one enticing island to another, enjoying the different beauty and culture of each location.

Serene Sunsets: There's nothing quite like seeing the sun fall below the horizon, painting the sky in bright shades of orange and pink, while you cruise down the Aegean coast. The peaceful seas and scenic scenery give the ideal background for breathtaking sunsets. Drop anchor in a peaceful harbor, enjoy a bottle of local wine, and see nature's stunning display as the day transitions into night.

Local Culture and Cuisine: Sailing the Aegean lets you to immerse yourself in the local culture and cuisine of the coastal cities and islands. Dock in scenic ports, visit lovely towns, and feast in delicious seafood at seaside tavernas. Experience the warm welcome of the inhabitants, learn about their traditions and customs, and experience the flavors of traditional Greek and Turkish meals.

Quiet Anchorages: Along the Aegean coast, you'll find various quiet anchorages where you may drop anchor and enjoy the tranquillity of unspoilt nature. These secret areas provide solitude and isolation, enabling you to rest, swim in clean waters, and soak up the sun in a serene atmosphere. It's the ideal chance to unplug from the rush and bustle of everyday life and experience the tranquillity of the sea.

Historical Sites: Sailing the Aegean coast gives a unique viewpoint on the region's rich history. From your boat, you may observe historical ruins, medieval fortresses, and archaeological sites that dot the coastline. Visit the ancient city of Ephesus, the temple of Apollo at Delphi, or the medieval castle of Bodrum, and experience the ruins of civilizations that have molded the Aegean area over the years.

Sailing the Aegean enables you to embrace the spirit of discovery and adventure while immersing yourself in the natural beauty, culture, and history of this enchanting area. Whether you opt to lease a boat, join a sailing tour, or pilot your own vessel, the Aegean's shoreline is yours to experience, one beautiful sight at a time. So go sail, feel the

wind in your hair, and let the Aegean Sea be your guide to
wonderful coastline discoveries.

CHAPTER 6

Gastronomy: A Culinary Journey around the Aegean

The Aegean area is not only a feast for the eyes with its breathtaking scenery and turquoise oceans but also a gastronomic paradise that tantalizes the taste senses with its rich tastes, fresh ingredients, and unique culinary traditions.

Embark on a culinary adventure throughout the Aegean and indulge in the delectable pleasures that define the region's rich food culture. From traditional Greek food to Turkish delicacies, here's an exhaustive tour of the gastronomy that awaits you in the Aegean:

Mediterranean Delights: The Aegean's culinary tapestry is profoundly based in Mediterranean cuisine, noted for its focus on fresh, seasonal ingredients and simple but tasty dishes. From sun-ripened tomatoes and juicy olives to aromatic herbs and delectable olive oil, the Mediterranean influence is present in every meal. Sample typical Greek mezze, such as tzatziki (yogurt and cucumber dip), dolmades (stuffed grape leaves), and fava (yellow split pea puree).

Embrace the Turkish tastes with meze plates with treats like hummus, babaganoush, and sigara borek (cheese-filled pastries).

Seafood Extravaganza: As a coastal location, the Aegean enjoys an abundance of seafood that takes center stage in many culinary dishes. Freshly caught fish, delicious shrimp, soft calamari, and plump mussels are hallmarks of the Aegean diet.

Enjoy grilled octopus coated with lemon and olive oil, relish a platter of fried anchovies or indulge in a seafood stew brimming with the scents of the sea. Each coastal town and island has its unique spin on seafood meals, enabling you to enjoy a range of regional delicacies.

Lamb and Goat Delicacies: In the Aegean, lamb and goat are valued meats that play a large part in traditional cuisines. From slow-roasted lamb shoulder to soft goat stew, these meats are cooked to perfection, frequently seasoned with fragrant herbs like rosemary, thyme, and oregano.

Don't miss the chance to eat "kokoretsi," a traditional delicacy made from lamb or goat offal wrapped in intestines and barbecued on a spit. The outcome is a delicious and luscious delicacy that demonstrates the Aegean's fondness for nose-to-tail cookery.

Cheese & Dairy Delights: The Aegean is recognized for its superb dairy products and a broad range of cheeses. Feta, derived from sheep's milk, is a mainstay in Greek cuisine, used in salads, pies, and as a topping for many foods.

Try the sour and creamy "tirokafteri," a spicy feta dip, or indulge in "saganaki," a fried cheese snack that's crunchy on the exterior and melty on the inside. You'll also find regional cheeses like "graviera," "kefalotyri," and "halloumi," each with its own particular qualities and tastes.

Olive Oil and Herbs: The Aegean is recognized for its great olive oil production, and it serves as the backbone of many meals in the area. Sample the delicious tastes of extra virgin olive oil poured over fresh salads, grilled vegetables, or as a finishing touch to grilled meats and seafood. Herbs like oregano, thyme, and rosemary are commonly employed, adding their particular scents and enriching the tastes of Aegean cuisine.

Sweet Temptations: No gastronomic excursion is complete without savoring in the sweet delicacies that adorn the Aegean's dessert tables. Try "baklava," a wonderful blend of phyllo pastry, nuts, and honey syrup. Sample the exquisite "Loukoumades," little doughnut-like balls drizzled with honey and dusted with cinnamon. And don't forget to try the traditional "halva," a semolina-based sweet flavored with nuts, spices, and fragrant extracts.

Wine and Spirits: The Aegean area is particularly famous for its winemaking heritage. Explore the vineyards and wineries that dot the countryside, and sample the broad variety of wines made in the area.

From crisp whites and fruity rosés to strong reds, Aegean wines provide a perfect complement to the local food. Additionally, indulge in a glass of "raki" or "ouzo," classic Greek and Turkish spirits, respectively, famed for their anise taste and consumed as a digestif.

As you begin on a gastronomic adventure throughout the Aegean, be prepared to stimulate your taste senses and explore the rich and unique tastes that distinguish this area. From the simplicity of Mediterranean food to the particular joys of local delicacies, the Aegean's gastronomy is likely to leave you with a profound appreciation for its culinary history.

Traditional Greek Cuisine: Delights of the Aegean

Greek food is famous internationally for its tastes, freshness, and rich culinary tradition. In the Aegean area, traditional Greek food takes on a distinct character, inspired by the richness of local products, the maritime lifestyle, and the cultural traditions that have molded the region's gastronomic pleasures.

Prepare to go on a gastronomic tour over the Aegean and delight in the classic Greek delicacies that will excite your taste buds:

Moussaka: A famous Greek meal, moussaka is a substantial casserole prepared with layers of eggplant, minced meat (typically lamb or beef), and a creamy béchamel sauce. The flavors mix together as it bakes to perfection, producing a warm and savory meal that captures the essence of Greek cuisine.

Souvlaki: A traditional Greek street cuisine, souvlaki consists of skewered and grilled meat (generally pig, chicken, or lamb) eaten with pita bread, tzatziki sauce, and a variety of accompaniments including tomatoes, onions, and fresh herbs.

The mix of succulent, marinated beef and the cooling tastes of tzatziki make souvlaki a popular and delicious alternative.

Greek Salad: Simple but delicious, Greek salad (Horiatiki) is a delightful combination of fresh tomatoes, cucumbers, red onions, bell peppers, olives, and feta cheese, drizzled with extra virgin olive oil and dusted with dried oregano. The brilliant colors and tastes of this salad encapsulate the spirit of Greek cuisine and the Aegean's sun-kissed fruit.

Spanakopita: A savory pastry, spanakopita highlights the Aegean's fondness for greens. It is constructed with layers of delicate phyllo dough filled with a blend of spinach, feta cheese, herbs, and onions. Baked till golden and crispy, spanakopita delivers a delicious blend of textures and tastes.

Dolmades: Dolmades are vine leaves loaded with a tasty blend of rice, herbs, and occasionally minced meat. These bite-sized delicacies are offered as appetizers or part of a mezze dish. The sour vine leaves, along with the fragrant filling, form a pleasant and delightful treat.

Baklava: A heavenly treat, baklava is a sweet pastry prepared with layers of thin phyllo dough, butter, and a variety of nuts (usually almonds, walnuts, or pistachios) sweetened with a spiced syrup. Each mouthful of this flaky and nutty treat is a taste of the Aegean's culinary history.

Taramasalata: A creamy and savory spread, taramasalata is created with fish roe (usually carp or cod), olive oil, lemon juice, and bread crumbs. It is served as a dip with bread or as part of a mezze dish. The acidic and briny tastes of taramasalata offer a distinctive touch to every dish.

Octopus: As a seaside location, the Aegean is famed for its wonderful octopus dishes. Grilled octopus, marinated in olive oil, lemon, and herbs, is a favorite in beach tavernas. Tender and tasty, octopus is a great joy for seafood fans.

Loukoumades: These bite-sized golden doughnuts are crispy on the surface, fluffy on the inside, and covered in honey syrup. Sprinkled with cinnamon and typically served with crushed almonds, Loukoumades are a lovely dessert and a beloved indulgence in the Aegean.

Ouzo: A ancient Greek liquor, ouzo is an anise-flavored drink that is frequently drunk as an aperitif or coupled with seafood. Its unique taste and perfume make it a mainstay in Greek culture and a vital element of any traditional Aegean dinner.

From the tastes of fresh ingredients to the rich and varied culinary traditions, traditional Greek cuisine in the Aegean is a celebration of simplicity, quality, and the enjoyment of excellent food.

Embark on this gastronomic trip and let the Aegean's culinary treasures take you to a world of unique sensations.

Local Specialties: Seafood, Olive Oil, and Feta Cheese

The Aegean area is endowed with a wealth of local delicacies that represent its coastal scenery, lush fields, and centuries-old culinary traditions. Among these delicacies, three stand out as emblems of Aegean cuisine: fish, olive oil, and feta cheese.

These ingredients not only form the basis of many traditional meals but also demonstrate the region's relationship to its natural resources and the skilled expertise that goes into crafting these culinary marvels.

Seafood: With its large coastline and closeness to the Aegean Sea, it's no wonder that seafood plays a big part in the Aegean's cuisine. Freshness is vital, and residents take pleasure in procuring the greatest seafood from the sea. From soft octopus to juicy shrimp, plump mussels to flaky salmon, the Aegean's seafood options are numerous and wonderful.

Grilled, baked, or fried, seafood meals are generally served simply to allow the natural tastes come through. Enjoy a platter of grilled sardines coated with lemon and olive oil, relish a seafood stew brimming with flavors, or indulge in a seafood pasta dish with the catch of the day.

Olive Oil: The Aegean is recognized for its great olive oil production, and the region's olive orchards generate some of the best oils in the world. Olive oil is not only a mainstay in Aegean cuisine but also an emblem of its cultural history. Known for its unique taste, rich scent, and health advantages, Aegean olive oil is used lavishly in cooking, dressing salads, and enhancing the flavors of numerous foods.

Whether it's dripping it over fresh vegetables, dipping bread into it, or using it as a foundation for marinades and sauces, the golden-green liquid gold of the Aegean is a crucial ingredient that lends depth and richness to the region's cuisine.

Feta Cheese: Feta cheese is a popular Greek cheese that has garnered international reputation. Made from sheep's milk or a mix of sheep and goat's milk, feta cheese is noted for its creamy texture, acidic taste, and crumbly consistency. In the Aegean, where sheep husbandry abounds, feta cheese maintains a unique position.

It is used in different cuisines, from classic Greek salads and spanakopita to stuffed peppers and cheese pies. The salty and briny overtones of feta cheese blend nicely with fresh vegetables, olives, and olive oil, providing a delicate balance of tastes that distinguishes Aegean cuisine.

When touring the Aegean, make sure to indulge in the region's distinctive delights. Taste the freshness of the sea in every mouthful of seafood, relish the rich and fragrant olive oil that enhances every meal, and feel the tangy creaminess of feta cheese that brings traditional Aegean dishes to life.

These local gems are not simply ingredients; they are a tribute to the Aegean's culinary legacy and the relationship between its people and the fertile land and sea that support them.

Food and Wine Festivals: Celebrating Aegean Flavors

Food and wine festivals in the Aegean region are colorful celebrations of the local culinary traditions, exhibiting the rich tastes, diversified ingredients, and cultural legacy of the area.

These events give a chance for both residents and tourists to immerse themselves in the Aegean's gourmet pleasures, explore traditional cooking skills, and appreciate the distinct flavors that distinguish the area. Let's examine some of the most prominent food and wine events that showcase Aegean flavors:

Ikaria Wine event (Ikaria Island, Greece): Held on the gorgeous island of Ikaria, this event commemorates the local wine production and the area's winemaking legacy. Visitors get the chance to try a range of wines created from indigenous grape varietals while enjoying live music, traditional dances, and local foods. The event displays the unique terroir of Ikaria and the devotion of its winemakers.

Bodrum International Gastronomy Festival (Bodrum, Turkey): Located in the Turkish Aegean, Bodrum holds an annual gastronomy festival that brings together famous chefs, food aficionados, and tourists from across the globe. The event showcases the diverse tastes of Turkish cuisine, with a concentration on Aegean delicacies. Attendees may enjoy in cooking demos, culinary seminars, and tastings, witnessing the culinary expertise and innovation of Turkish chefs.

Tinos Food Paths (Tinos Island, Greece): Tinos Island is famed for its distinct gastronomic culture, and the Tinos Food Paths festival is a celebration of the island's culinary traditions. The festival provides a tour through Tinos' native goods, including artisanal cheeses, cured meats, honey, and the island's famed "tzaleta" (sun-dried tomatoes). Visitors may engage in cuisine seminars, attend cooking demos, and sample the island's traditional meals made by local chefs.

International Izmir Kordon Fish event (Izmir, Turkey): Located in Izmir, a bustling city on the Aegean coast of Turkey, this event commemorates the region's rich seafood tradition. The festival features a broad range of locally caught fish and seafood dishes, cooked by professional chefs from the area. Visitors may enjoy sampling sessions, cookery displays, and live music while taking in the exciting ambiance of the festival.

Lesvos Food and Wine Festival (Lesvos Island, Greece): Lesvos Island is famed for its olive oil, ouzo, and distinctive local goods. The Lesvos Food and Wine Festival is an annual event that brings together local producers, wineries, and chefs to exhibit the island's gourmet delights. Visitors may experience a broad choice of local foods, including the famed "sardelles pastes" (anchovy pastes), traditional sweets, and locally made wines.

Samos Wine Festival (Samos Island, Greece): Samos Island is famed for its sweet wine production, and the Samos Wine Festival honors this old heritage. The festival takes place in the town of Karlovasi and features wine tastings, vineyard excursions, and cultural activities. Visitors may taste the distinctive aromas of Samos' sweet Muscat wines, complimented by traditional Aegean food.

These food and wine events offer an immersive experience for visitors looking to dig into the Aegean's gastronomic legacy. They give an opportunity to try regional delicacies, learn about local food production, and meet with enthusiastic farmers and chefs. Whether you're a food fanatic, a wine lover, or just interested about the tastes of the Aegean, visiting these festivals will be a remarkable voyage through the region's rich culinary and cultural traditions.

CHAPTER 7

Mythology and Legends: Unveiling Greece's Ancient Stories

Mythology and legends constitute an intrinsic part of Greece's complex cultural fabric, and the Aegean area, with its historical importance and ancient legacy, is a treasure mine of enthralling stories.

Exploring the myths and tales of Greece is like going on a voyage into the land of gods, heroes, and mythological creatures, unraveling the stories that have influenced the Greek psyche for ages. Let us explore into the intriguing realm of Greek mythology and stories that decorate the landscapes of the Aegean:

The Olympian Gods: Mount Olympus, the tallest peak in Greece and the mythological residence site of the gods, is situated near the Aegean shoreline. According to Greek mythology, the twelve Olympian gods, headed by Zeus, reigned over the earth from this holy mountain. Discover the tales of Zeus, Hera, Poseidon, Athena, Apollo, and other gods and goddesses whose lives and activities were entwined with human events.

The Trojan War: The Trojan War, one of the most recognized tales in Greek mythology, is situated in the Aegean area. The conflict between the Greeks and the Trojans, initiated by the kidnapping of Helen, the wife of Menelaus, by Prince Paris of Troy, has captured the imagination of humanity for millennia. Explore the famous city of Troy, see the archaeological site, and immerse yourself in the epic legends of heroes like Achilles, Hector, and Odysseus.

The Odyssey: The Odyssey, credited to the author Homer, is an epic poem that chronicles the adventures of Odysseus (Ulysses) as he strives to return home after the Trojan War. The Aegean Sea serves as the background for his lengthy and arduous trip, as he sees fabled animals, navigates difficult waters, and endures countless hardships. Visit the island of Ithaca, considered to be Odysseus' homeland, and follow the footsteps of this famous hero.

The Minotaur and the Labyrinth: The island of Crete, situated in the Aegean Sea, is steeped in myth and legend. One of the most famous myths is that of the Minotaur, a half-human, half-bull beast who dwelt in the labyrinth under the palace of King Minos at Knossos. Discover the relics of the Minoan culture at the Palace of Knossos and immerse yourself in the mythology of Theseus, who journeyed into the labyrinth to slaughter the Minotaur.

The Sirens: According to Greek mythology, the Sirens were alluring monsters whose seductive sounds led sailors to their fate. These fabled people inhabited on rocky islands in the Aegean Sea, enticing passing sailors with their enchanting singing. Sail down the Aegean coast and experience the haunting music of the Sirens as you explore the lovely islands.

Medusa and Perseus: The story of Medusa, the Gorgon with snakes for hair, and her meeting with the hero Perseus is a tale of courage and adventure. Medusa's head was thought to possess the ability to turn everyone who stared at her into stone. Discover the ties between Medusa and the Aegean area, particularly the island of Seriphos, where Perseus was claimed to have been reared.

The Birthplace of Aphrodite: According to Greek mythology, the goddess of love and beauty, Aphrodite (Venus), was born from the sea foam on the island of Cyprus, which sits in the eastern part of the Aegean Sea.

Explore the legendary links of Aphrodite and explore locations linked with her, such as the Baths of Aphrodite in Paphos, where she was reported to have showered.

These are only a few instances of the intriguing myths and folklore that pervade the Aegean area.

Exploring these ancient myths and their ties to the landscapes and archaeological sites of the Aegean adds an added depth of fascination to every visit. Immerse yourself in the myths and legends of Greece, and let the ancient stories weave their spell, taking you to a world where gods and heroes once roamed the Aegean coasts.

The Legends of Mount Olympus: Home of the Gods

Mount Olympus, looming magnificently in northern Greece, is not simply a physical mountain but also a legendary region that retains tremendous importance in Greek mythology. Known as the abode place of the gods, this famous mountain is wrapped in legends of power, love, treachery, and courage.

The stories of Mount Olympus give a look into the complicated lives of the Olympian gods and their relationships with humanity. Let us discover some of the interesting mythology related with Mount Olympus:

The Birth of the Gods: According to Greek mythology, the gods were born to the Titan gods Cronus and Rhea. In dread of being ousted by his progeny, Cronus swallowed each of his babies. However, Rhea managed to preserve their youngest son, Zeus, by concealing him on Mount Dikte in Crete. When Zeus grew up, he returned to Mount Olympus and organized an uprising against Cronus, finally becoming the king of the gods.

The Twelve Olympian Gods: Mount Olympus served as the heavenly dwelling of the twelve principal gods and goddesses that constituted the Olympian pantheon. Zeus, the ruler of the gods, presided over the mountain and its heavenly people. Other important deities were Hera, Zeus' wife and queen of the gods; Poseidon, the god of the sea; Athena, the goddess of wisdom; Apollo, the god of the sun; and Aphrodite, the goddess of love.

The Divine Council: Mount Olympus was not only the abode of the gods but also the meeting location for their divine council. Here, the Olympian gods would gather to debate important topics, make judgments, and interfere in the affairs of mankind. The council's debates and choices molded the future of both gods and mortals, reflecting the divine order and balance of the cosmos.

Zeus and His Love relationships: Zeus, famed for his countless love relationships, frequently descended from Mount Olympus in the shape of various animals or people to pursue his amorous interests.

These excursions led in the development of countless demi-gods and mythological animals. For example, Zeus changed into a swan to seduce Leda, a mortal woman, culminating to the birth of Helen of Troy. His love relationships and exploits produced drama, envy, and war among the gods.

Heavenly Interventions: Mount Olympus was the focus of heavenly power, and the gods regularly interfered in the lives of mankind. They impacted human affairs, provided blessings, or administered penalties. The interactions between gods and humans emphasized the delicate balance between destiny and free choice, underlining the repercussions of human acts and the role of the gods in creating destinies.

The Titanomachy: Before the reign of the Olympian gods, a tremendous conflict known as the Titanomachy took place between the Titans, who reigned before the Olympians, and the Olympian gods. This epic fight transpired on Mount Olympus, with the gods finally emerging triumphant and sending the vanquished Titans to Tartarus, a deep pit.

The stories of Mount Olympus not only portray the dynamic interactions among the gods but also mirror the intricacies of human nature, exhibiting themes of love, power, morality, and fate. They give insights into the ideals, beliefs, and goals of ancient Greek culture, highlighting the connection between the divine and mortal spheres.

Today, Mount Olympus continues to inspire amazement and curiosity. Its steep peaks, lush woods, and spectacular panoramas serve as a reminder of the fabled region that once captured the minds of the ancient Greeks. Exploring the stories of Mount Olympus enables us to plunge into a world where gods ruled supreme and humans aspired for their favor, reminding us of the continuing power and attraction of Greek mythology.

Homer's Odyssey: Tracing the Epic Journey

Homer's Odyssey is an ancient Greek epic poem that relates the account of Odysseus' hard voyage home after the Trojan War. Filled with adventure, mythology, and heroic encounters, the Odyssey is a riveting story that has lasted the test of time.

Tracing the legendary odyssey of Odysseus enables us to plunge into a realm of mythological animals, captivating encounters, and the persistence of the human spirit. Let us go on this incredible odyssey:

Departure from Troy: The Odyssey starts with Odysseus and his allies fleeing from the ruined city of Troy, where they had conducted a long and hard battle. Their primary purpose is to return home to Ithaca, but their voyage is plagued with hardships and impediments, both natural and supernatural.

The Cyclops and the Land of the Lotus Eaters: One of the most remarkable incidents in the Odyssey is the meeting with Polyphemus, the Cyclops. Odysseus and his crew find themselves imprisoned in the Cyclops' cave and must outsmart the monster to escape. Afterward, they journey to the country of the Lotus Eaters, where they discover a tribe that feasts on the lotus fruit, forcing them to forget their desire to return home.

Circe's Enchantment: Odysseus and his crew reach the island of Aeaea, where they meet the enchantress Circe. Through her magical abilities, Circe converts some of Odysseus' soldiers into pigs. However, with the assistance of the god Hermes, Odysseus fights Circe's charm and finally earns her affection. They spend a year on the island before resuming their trek.

The Sirens and Scylla and Charybdis: As Odysseus and his men sail through the island of the Sirens, he has his crew block their ears with wax to prevent being enticed to their deaths by the Sirens' alluring melodies.

They then confront the hazardous strait between Scylla, a gigantic sea creature, and Charybdis, a lethal whirlpool. Odysseus must make a tough decision between the two hazards.

Calypso's Island: After surviving countless challenges, Odysseus washes ashore on the island of Ogygia, where he is kept hostage by the nymph Calypso. For seven years, Odysseus stays confined on the island, wanting to return home. Eventually, with the assistance of the gods, he is liberated and continues his trip.

The Return to Ithaca: Odysseus eventually reaches on the beaches of his country, Ithaca, but he must endure more trials before he can retake his kingdom. He disguises himself as a beggar and devises a plot to rid his house of the suitors fighting for his wife Penelope's hand. After a spectacular struggle, Odysseus exposes his actual identity and reunites with his family.

Homer's Odyssey is not just a narrative of adventure but also an examination of the human condition. It explores on issues of loyalty, endurance, and the desire for home. Odysseus' trip serves as a metaphor for the hardships and tribulations of life, where one must navigate through difficulties, encounter temptations, and find the fortitude to conquer adversity.

The Odyssey's lasting appeal stems in its universal themes and ageless narrative. It continues to capture readers with its colorful images, intriguing characters, and the feeling of wonder it generates.

Tracing the legendary voyage of Odysseus helps us to immerse ourselves in the realm of ancient Greek mythology, revealing the layers of adventure, courage, and the search for homecoming.

Mythical Islands: Tales of the Aegean Sea

The Aegean Sea, with its sparkling blue waves and dispersed archipelagos, has long been a source of inspiration for myths and tales. Within this fabled expanse, several islands have grabbed the imagination of writers and travelers alike. Let us begin on a tour over the Aegean Sea as we examine 10 fabled islands and the legends related with them:

Atlantis: The fabled island of Atlantis, recounted by Plato, is claimed to have been a highly sophisticated society that sunk under the sea in a single day and night of devastating devastation. The actual site of Atlantis remains a mystery, however many estimate it to be located inside the Aegean Sea.

Delos: Delos, a little island in the Cyclades, possesses tremendous legendary importance. According to Greek mythology, it is the birthplace of the twin gods Apollo and Artemis. Delos was regarded to be a holy island, and its shrine devoted to Apollo drew visitors from far and wide.

Lesbos: Lesbos, noted for its natural beauty, is connected with the ancient Greek poet Sappho, who was born on the island. Sappho's lyrical poetry, notably her confessions of love and longing for women, have made her a symbol of female homosexuality, giving origin to the name "lesbian."

Samothrace: Samothrace, an isolated island in the northeastern Aegean, was the location of the ancient mystery religion of the Great Gods. This secretive religion revolved upon secret initiation rites and rituals, and the island was regarded a hallowed site of spiritual importance.

Naxos: In Greek mythology, Naxos is famed as the island where Theseus abandoned Ariadne, the princess who had helped him cross the maze of the Minotaur. The island's stunning surroundings and lovely communities contribute to its attraction.

Kos: The island of Kos is linked with the mythical character of Hippocrates, regarded as the "Father of Medicine." Hippocrates, who was born on Kos, created a school of medicine and formulated the Hippocratic Oath, which remains an ethical guide for doctors to this day.

Patmos: Patmos is notable for being the island where the apostle John received the heavenly revelations that formed the foundation of the Book of Revelation in the Bible. The Cave of the Apocalypse, a religious place on Patmos, is considered to be the spot where John had his visions.

Lemnos: Lemnos is associated to the tale of the Amazons, a band of warrior women. According to tradition, the island served as a haven for the Amazons and was controlled by Queen Hippolyta. Lemnos also has ties with the deity Hephaestus, who was thought to have fallen from Mount Olympus and landed on the island.

Thasos: Thasos is claimed to have been inhabited by the satyr Silenus, the instructor and companion of the deity Dionysus. The island was noted for its beautiful flora, mineral resources, and wine production, making it intimately related to Dionysian festivals.

Aegina: Aegina, situated in the Saronic Gulf, was named for the nymph Aegina, who was stolen by Zeus and became the mother of the hero Aeacus. The island was a significant marine and trade hub in ancient times.

These mythological islands of the Aegean Sea continue to captivate and inspire, their traditions woven into the fabric of Greek culture and history. Exploring their coasts is not only a chance to wallow in natural beauty but also an opportunity to immerse oneself in the myths and magical tales that have defined the area for millennia.

CHAPTER 8

Natural Wonders: Exploring the Aegean's Landscapes

The Aegean area is not only recognized for its rich history and cultural legacy but also for its spectacular natural features.

From stunning coasts and lovely islands to steep mountains and verdant valleys, the Aegean provides a broad spectrum of natural beauties ready to be discovered. In this chapter, we will dig into the stunning landscapes of the Aegean, leading you through its outstanding characteristics and showcasing the greatest sites for nature enthusiasts.

Coastal Splendors

The Aegean shoreline provides some of the most beautiful vistas in the world. With its crystal-clear turquoise seas, beautiful sandy beaches, and spectacular cliffs, it's a dream for beach aficionados and water sports enthusiasts alike.

From the renowned beaches of Mykonos and Santorini to the hidden treasures of Paros and Naxos, each coastal resort provides a distinct charm and beauty.

Majestic Mountains

The Aegean is not only about the water; it also includes spectacular mountain ranges that provide stunning panoramas and exhilarating experiences. Mount Olympus, the mythological residence of the gods, stands as the tallest peak in Greece and encourages hikers and mountaineers to conquer its routes. Explore the harsh terrain of the Pelion Peninsula or travel to the awe-inspiring Samaria Gorge in Crete for a unique trekking adventure.

Enchanting Forests and Valleys

Beyond the beaches and mountains, the Aegean area is home to lovely woods and green valleys. Explore the lush pine woods of Mount Taygetos in the Peloponnese or meander through the olive fields of Lesvos Island. Discover secret waterfalls in the Epirus area or immerse yourself in the peacefulness of the Valley of the Butterflies near Rhodes.

Captivating Caves

The Aegean is peppered with captivating caverns, allowing a look into the deep mysteries of nature.

The Blue caverns in Zakynthos with its iridescent blue waters, the Melissani Cave in Kefalonia with its subterranean lake, and the Cave of the Apocalypse in

Patmos, where Saint John authored the Book of Revelation, are just a few examples of the interesting caverns waiting to be discovered.

Protected Natural Parks and Reserves

The Aegean is devoted to protecting its natural resources, and various national parks and protected areas have been created to maintain its distinct ecosystems.

Visit the Alonissos Marine Park, a home for unique marine life, or explore the Dilek Peninsula-Büyük Menderes Delta National Park, famed for its numerous bird species. These protected areas give an opportunity to immerse yourself in unspoiled nature and see the region's biodiversity.

Hiking & Nature Trails: Discovering the Aegean's Wilderness

The Aegean area of Greece provides a wealth of natural beauty and different landscapes that are great for trekking enthusiasts and wildlife lovers.

From rough mountains to lush forests, and from isolated beaches to secret valleys, the Aegean's wildness is a treasure trove waiting to be discovered. Lace up your hiking boots and get ready to start on a trek across the region's intriguing paths and immerse yourself in its breathtaking natural treasures.

Mount Olympus: As the tallest mountain in Greece, Mount Olympus is a hiker's dream. Its towering slopes are home to a great diversity of flora and animals, and the paths give stunning views of the surrounding area. Hiking to the peak of Mount Olympus is a demanding but rewarding journey, enabling you to observe the awe-inspiring splendor that inspired ancient Greek mythology.

Samaria Gorge: Located in Crete, the Samaria Gorge is one of Europe's longest and most intriguing valleys. The path travels past high cliffs, aromatic pine trees, and crystal-clear streams, delivering a spectacular hiking journey. As you explore the canyon, keep a look out for rare types of fauna including the characteristic Cretan wild goats known as krikri.

Vikos Gorge: Situated in the Zagori area of Epirus, Vikos Gorge is famed for its startling depth and stunning limestone cliffs. This UNESCO-recognized canyon provides a great hiking experience, with routes that wind through lush flora, historic stone bridges, and quaint medieval towns.

Take in the awe-inspiring vistas from the vantage points along the route, and marvel at the raw beauty of this natural masterpiece.

Nisyros Volcano: The island of Nisyros, situated in the Dodecanese, is home to a dormant volcano that provides a unique trekking experience. The walk leads you through strange scenery, including colorful volcanic craters, hot fumaroles, and lunar-like terrain.

Hiking on Nisyros enables you to observe the strong forces of nature up close and admire the island's geological beauties.

Chios Mastiha Trails: The island of Chios is famed for its production of mastiha, a natural resin with numerous applications. The Chios Mastiha Trails lead you across the southern half of the island, where you may stroll among the mastic trees and explore the rich history and cultivation practices of this unique product. The paths provide a blend of natural beauty, cultural legacy, and pleasant smells.

Mount Athos: Located on the Athos Peninsula in northern Greece, Mount Athos is a UNESCO World Heritage Site and a cherished spiritual destination for Orthodox Christians. While admission to the monastic community is limited to male pilgrims, trekking around the circumference of the peninsula affords beautiful views of the monasteries, the turquoise seas of the Aegean Sea, and the pristine natural environs.

Amorgos Trails: The island of Amorgos, in the Cyclades, has a network of well-marked trails that enable you to explore its rough terrain, medieval towns, and exquisite beaches. From the lovely town of Chora to the scenic hamlet of Tholaria and the monastery of Panagia Hozoviotissa, trekking on Amorgos is a great opportunity to immerse yourself in the island's original charm.

Rhodes Valley of the Butterflies: The Valley of the Butterflies, situated in Rhodes, is a quiet paradise that acts as a refuge for the Jersey Tiger Moth butterflies throughout the summer months. The paths travel through a beautiful wooded valley, passing through streams, waterfalls, and wooden bridges. This fascinating stroll enables you to watch the bright butterflies in their natural environment and savor the peacefulness of the surroundings.

Mount Pelion: Situated in Thessaly, Mount Pelion provides a broad selection of hiking paths that go through deep woods, green meadows, and historic stone-built towns. The mountain is notable for its mythical ties, since it was considered to be the home of the centaurs.

Hiking on Mount Pelion enables you to experience the harmonious combination of mountain and sea, as the routes give beautiful views of the Aegean shoreline.

Alonissos Marine Park: Alonissos, a tiny island in the Sporades, is home to the first declared marine park in Greece. Hiking around the island's pathways enables you to discover the pure natural surroundings, including the thick pine woods and rough shoreline. Keep a watch out for the endangered Mediterranean monk seals that inhabit the marine park, as well as a variety of bird species.

Before beginning on any hiking expedition, it's necessary to be prepared and equipped with adequate gear, including durable hiking shoes, a map, and sufficient water and food.

It's also important to verify weather conditions and path difficulty levels, since certain routes may demand a particular degree of fitness and expertise. With its various landscapes and enticing pathways, the Aegean's wildness welcomes people who want an immersive and satisfying outdoor experience.

Samaria Gorge: A Journey across a Natural Wonder

Located on the island of Crete, the Samaria Gorge is an awe-inspiring natural beauty that draws hikers and wildlife lovers from across the globe.

Stretching over 16 kilometers (10 miles) in length, this spectacular canyon is not only one of the longest gorges in Europe but also a protected national park and a UNESCO Biosphere Reserve.

Embarking on a trek through the Samaria Gorge provides a memorable hiking experience, immersing you in its raw beauty and intriguing vistas.

The trip starts near the settlement of Omalos, where the trailhead marks the entrance to the gorge.

As you walk onto the route, you are instantly welcomed with towering cliffs, thick flora, and the sound of the untamed waterways that have cut their way down the canyon over thousands of years. The route lowers gently, taking you further into the heart of the canyon.

Throughout the journey, you'll see a diversity of beautiful landscapes and natural structures. The narrowest section of the canyon, known as the "Iron Gates," provides a spectacular view as the cliffs loom above, producing a feeling of awe and amazement.

The walk takes you down the riverbank, where crystal-clear rivers run and form little pools and waterfalls, giving a pleasant rest along the way.

As you explore the gorge, keep a look out for the different plants and wildlife that make this unique environment home. The Samaria Gorge is home to various indigenous plant species, including the uncommon Cretan wild goat or kri-kri, which may make an appearance along the walk.

Birdwatchers will enjoy rejoice in the possibility to view many bird species, including the bearded vulture and golden eagle.

One of the most impressive qualities of the Samaria Gorge is the feeling of tranquility and seclusion it creates. As you venture further into the canyon, the outer world melts away, and you find yourself immersed in the pure nature. The tranquillity of the surroundings enables you to connect with nature, giving a reprieve from the hurry and bustle of daily life.

Reaching the conclusion of the trek, you'll emerge at the little seaside hamlet of Agia Roumeli, where the Libyan Sea awaits. Take a minute to bask in the splendor of the pebble beaches and turquoise seas, delivering a well-deserved reward for finishing the walk.

 Enjoy a refreshing dip or relax in one of the coastal tavernas, relishing local specialities and reminiscing on the fantastic voyage you've just completed.

It's vital to remember that climbing the Samaria Gorge demands a reasonable degree of fitness, since the terrain may be tough and uneven in certain areas. Proper footwear, sun protection, and lots of water are crucial for a pleasant and safe trek.

Additionally, it's essential to examine the opening hours and seasonal availability of the gorge, since it is closed during some months to conserve the sensitive habitat.

Embarking on a tour through the Samaria Gorge is an experience that enables you to observe the raw force of nature and immerse yourself in the wild beauty of Crete. From its towering cliffs and lush landscapes to its serene tranquillity, the canyon gives a look into the everlasting glories of the natural world, leaving an unforgettable mark on everyone who wander inside its depths.

Volcanic Marvels: Nisyros and the Santorini Caldera

The Aegean area of Greece is not only famed for its magnificent scenery and crystal-clear seas but also for its interesting volcanic activity. Two excellent examples of this volcanic wonder are the island of Nisyros and the Santorini Caldera. Let's explore into these unusual sites and find the geological marvels they offer.

Nisyros: Nestled in the Dodecanese, the little island of Nisyros is a hidden treasure that has a volcanic environment like no other. Its greatest attraction is the dormant volcano, which last erupted over 20,000 years ago. The volcanic activity has altered the island's landscape, producing a strange setting that captivates tourists.

One of the features of Nisyros is the Stefanos Crater, situated near the hamlet of Nikia. This spectacular crater portrays the sheer force of nature, with its gushing sulfur springs and steaming fumaroles. The views from the crater rim are incredibly magnificent, enabling you to watch the volcanic processes that have sculpted the island.

Exploring Nisyros further, you'll meet the lovely town of Mandraki, where old whitewashed cottages and tiny winding alleyways create a wonderful ambience. Don't miss the chance to visit the island's volcano museum, which gives insights into the geological history of Nisyros and the volcanic processes that have sculpted the island.

Santorini Caldera: Santorini is arguably one of the most famous and sought-after places in the Aegean Sea, and its volcanic origins play a key part in its attraction. The island is part of a larger volcanic complex known as the Santorini Caldera, which was produced by a catastrophic volcanic eruption approximately 3,500 years ago.

The caldera is a vast submerged crater, encircled by high cliffs that give panoramic views of the Aegean Sea. The whitewashed structures of Santorini's iconic cliffside villages, such as Fira and Oia, cling to the volcanic cliffs, producing a postcard-perfect sight that has become associated with the island.

Exploring the Santorini Caldera enables you to view the remarkable geological structures that arose from the past eruption. One significant landmark is the island of Nea Kameni, nestled inside the caldera. Here, you may trek to the peak of the volcano, where you'll be rewarded with awe-inspiring panoramas of the neighboring islands and the deep blue oceans below.

Another noteworthy part of the caldera is the island of Palea Kameni, noted for its thermal hot springs. Taking a swim in the warm waters is not only a pleasant experience but also a chance to appreciate the medicinal powers connected with the mineral-rich volcanic springs.

Whether you visit Nisyros or tour the Santorini Caldera, you'll be treated to a unique and intriguing experience that shows the strength and beauty of volcanic activity. These places provide a view into the geological processes that have sculpted the Aegean area and provide a greater knowledge of the natural treasures that make Greece such a wonderful place to visit.

CHAPTER 9

Cultural Immersion: Festivals and Traditions

Cultural immersion is a crucial component of traveling, enabling you to engage with the local population, experience their customs, and develop a greater knowledge of their way of life.

In the Aegean area of Greece, cultural immersion is a rich and vivid experience, with several festivals and customs that give a window into the region's cultural legacy. Let's examine some of the most notable festivals and customs that might enrich your cultural immersion adventure in the Aegean.

Easter Celebrations: Easter is one of the most prominent religious holidays in Greece, and the Aegean area is no exception when it comes to commemorating this important occasion.

From the processions of the epitaph (a representation of Christ's tomb) through the streets to the midnight church service and the traditional Easter Sunday feast, participating in Easter festivities allows you to witness the deep-rooted religious traditions and experience the sense of community that comes with this joyous occasion.

Panigiri Festivals: Panigiri festivals are vivid festivities that take place in numerous villages and towns throughout the Aegean islands throughout the year. These festivals are a blend of religious and cultural activities, with live music, traditional dancing, and an abundance of local food and drink.

Attending a panigiri festival gives an opportunity to immerse oneself in the vibrant environment, connect with residents, and join in the festivities that exhibit the region's unique character.

Traditional Music and Dance: The Aegean islands have a rich musical past, with traditional music and dance playing a crucial part in local culture. From the bright and rhythmic sounds of the bouzouki to the intense and complicated movements of traditional dances like the syrtos and the hasapiko, watching a live performance of traditional music and dance is an immersive cultural experience that gets you closer to the heart of Aegean traditions.

Wine Harvest Festivals: The Aegean area is famed for its wine production, and the harvest season brings about a number of wine festivals and festivities. These events are a terrific chance to try local wines, observe traditional grape stomping, and participate in wine-related activities.

Participating in a wine harvest festival enables you to enjoy the region's winemaking tradition, learn about the production process, and experience the flavors of Aegean wines.

Traditional Crafts and artists: Exploring the Aegean area affords opportunity to explore traditional crafts and artists who continue to preserve old traditions alive. From pottery and weaving to woodcarving and jewelry creation, witnessing these talented artists at work and learning about their profession gives insight into the region's creative legacy. You may even get the opportunity to try your hand at a traditional skill via workshops and interactive experiences.

Religious Pilgrimages: The Aegean is littered with monasteries, churches, and religious places that possess considerable cultural and historical relevance. Many of these locations draw pilgrims from near and far, particularly during religious festivals and feast days. Joining a pilgrimage enables you to observe the great commitment and spirituality of the people, engage in religious events, and develop a better respect for the religious traditions that have influenced the area.

Traditional Cuisine: Food is a vital element of every culture, and the Aegean area provides a rich gastronomic legacy. From classic Greek meals like moussaka and souvlaki to regional delicacies like fresh seafood, local cheeses, and sweet delights like loukoumades, indulging in the tastes of Aegean cuisine is a great way to immerse yourself in the local culture.

Engaging in these festivals, rituals, and cultural events delivers an immersive journey into the core of the Aegean's cultural history.

It helps you to form ties with the local people, get insights into their customs, and develop lasting recollections that go beyond basic sightseeing. Embrace the chance to participate, study, and rejoice with the Aegean people, and you'll walk away with a better awareness for the region's cultural diversity.

Festivals of the Aegean: Dancing, Music, and Revelry

The Aegean area of Greece is famed for its vivid festivals, which are marked by enthusiastic dancing, energetic music, and cheerful celebration. These festivals give a look into the rich cultural legacy of the area, where traditions are honored with great passion and pride.

From religious processions to folklore celebrations, the festivals of the Aegean generate an atmosphere of mirth and friendship. Let's examine some of the important festivals that exhibit the dancing, music, and merriment of the Aegean.

Klapa Festival (Hydra): Held annually on the scenic island of Hydra, the Klapa Festival is a celebration of traditional Greek music. Klapa refers to a kind of acapella singing that developed in the Dalmatian area of Croatia and has significant links to the Greek island culture.

During the festival, skilled musicians and singers come to play klapa songs, filling the air with their pleasant sounds. Visitors get the chance to see mesmerizing performances and immerse themselves in the wonderful sounds of Greek music.

Festival of the Aegean (Syros): Syros, the capital of the Cyclades, holds the famous Festival of the Aegean every summer. This worldwide cultural festival brings together brilliant performers from Greece and beyond to display their abilities in music, opera, theater, and dance. The event takes place in numerous locations around the island, including ancient theaters and open-air amphitheaters. Audiences are exposed to spectacular performances, emphasizing the variety and creative brilliance of the Aegean area.

Feast of the Assumption (Tinos): Tinos is noted for its intense religious devotion, and the Feast of the Assumption is one of the most major religious celebrations on the island. On the 15th of August, hundreds of pilgrims gather to Tinos to offer honor to the Virgin Mary.

The festivities feature a magnificent parade when the icon of the Virgin Mary is carried through the streets, attended by priests, residents, and tourists. Traditional music and dance contribute to the celebratory mood, creating a cheerful and respectful ambience.

Karpathian Wedding Festival (Karpathos): The Karpathian Wedding Festival is a unique cultural event that reenacts traditional Karpathian wedding rituals.

This boisterous celebration takes place in the hamlet of Olympos and includes the whole community, dressed in vivid traditional costumes. The celebrations include traditional dances, music performances, and theatrical displays that reflect the many phases of a Karpathian wedding. Visitors may immerse themselves in the exuberant celebration and witness the preservation of age-old practices.

International Dance Festival (Chania): The city of Chania in Crete organizes the International Dance Festival, which brings together dancers from various nations to demonstrate their ability and share cultural expressions via dance. The event covers a broad spectrum of dance forms, from traditional folk dances to modern acts.

The streets and squares of Chania come alive with vivid colors, music, and rhythm as dancers from diverse cultures join together to produce a dazzling show of movement and creative expression.

Attending these festivals enables you to observe the power of music and dance in bringing communities together, honoring their history, and developing a feeling of belonging. It's a chance to experience the energy, passion, and creativity that pervade the Aegean culture. Whether you find yourself tapping your feet to traditional Greek rhythms, engaging in the dance circles, or just enjoying the vivid atmosphere, these festivals will leave you with lasting memories and a better understanding for the cultural diversity of the Aegean area.

Traditional Crafts and Artisans: Preserving Ancient Techniques

Traditional crafts and artists play a crucial role in conserving the cultural legacy and traditional methods of the Aegean area. Through their artistry, these talented people maintain alive the traditions handed down through centuries, producing unique and true pieces of art.

From pottery and weaving to woodwork and metalwork, the traditional crafts of the Aegean are a tribute to the region's rich history and cultural identity. Let's examine some of the classic crafts and the people that are devoted to maintaining these historical traditions.

Pottery: Pottery making has a long history in the Aegean, extending back thousands of years. Skilled potters produce stunning ceramics using traditions handed down through centuries. In the island of Sifnos, for example, the skill of pottery-making is profoundly established in the local culture.

Artisans form clay with their hands or on a potter's wheel, turning it into different containers and ornamental pieces. The pottery is then burned in kilns using ancient processes, resulting in unique pieces that represent the island's past.

Weaving and Textiles: The skill of weaving and textile manufacture is another historic trade that flourishes in the Aegean. In regions like Crete and Tinos, experienced weavers make exquisite fabrics using looms and ancient processes.

They work with local resources, such as wool and cotton, to manufacture woven textiles, carpets, tapestries, and other textile goods. These artists typically combine traditional patterns and motifs, bringing a touch of cultural meaning to their products.

Woodwork: Woodwork is a craft that exhibits the expertise and craftsmanship of Aegean artists. In Rhodes, for instance, woodcarving is profoundly rooted in the island's heritage. Skilled artisans carve beautiful motifs on furniture, doors, and other objects using locally available wood. The workmanship typically includes traditional themes and aspects, making each item a unique work of art.

Metalwork: The craft of metalwork has been performed in the Aegean area for ages. In locales like Santorini and Mykonos, experienced metalworkers make magnificent jewelry, sculptures, and decorative objects using traditional methods. They work with metals like silver, copper, and bronze, utilizing age-old procedures like as hammering, soldering, and filigree work to produce complex and elegant creations.

Icon Painting: Icon painting is a cherished and treasured practice in the Greek Orthodox Church. Skilled iconographers produce religious icons, following precise procedures and symbolic traditions. The icons, generally painted on wood panels, portray saints, religious themes, and biblical characters.

Artists methodically add layers of paint and gold leaf, using traditional colors and natural materials. This old craft is a monument to the spiritual and cultural history of the Aegean.

Preserving these old crafts demands devotion and a strong grasp of the cultural importance underlying each skill. Artisans in the Aegean area take pleasure in their work, frequently transmitting their expertise and abilities to subsequent generations. Their devotion to conserving traditional skills guarantees that these crafts continue to flourish and contribute to the region's cultural diversity.

Visiting the workshops and studios of these craftsmen gives a chance to observe their creation firsthand and learn about the traditional methods they apply. You may appreciate their artistry, acquire unique handcrafted things, and support the continuance of these traditional trades. By recognizing and appreciating these ancient crafts and craftsmen, we contribute to the preservation of the Aegean's cultural legacy for years to come.

Cultural Etiquette: Embracing Greek Customs and Traditions

When going to the Aegean area of Greece, it's crucial to learn and accept the cultural practices and traditions of the local people. By respecting and partaking in these customs, you may enrich your travel experience and encourage pleasant relationships with the people. Here are some cultural etiquette recommendations to assist you manage Greek customs and traditions:

Greetings and Hospitality: Greeks are famed for their great hospitality. When welcoming someone, it is usual to give a cordial handshake, followed by direct eye contact. Greeks generally participate in impassioned discussion, and it's usual to see people kissing each other on the cheeks, particularly among friends and relatives.

If welcomed into someone's house, it is courteous to offer a modest present, such as cookies or a bottle of wine, as a sign of thanks.

Respect for Religion: Greece has a deep relationship to the Greek Orthodox Church, and religion plays a large part in everyday life. When visiting churches or monasteries, it is vital to dress modestly and politely, covering your shoulders and knees. Avoid loud discussions and respect the solemnity of the area. Additionally, be mindful of religious holidays and festivals, since they may alter local traditions and services.

Table Manners and Dining: Greek food is a vital component of the cultural experience, and eating meals with people is a regular activity. When dining in Greece, it's customary to wait for the host to welcome you to start eating. It is typical to use utensils for most foods, however certain traditional meals, like as meze (small plates), may be eaten with your hands. Tipping is traditional in restaurants, often approximately 10% of the bill, as a token of gratitude for the service.

"Filoxenia" - The Greek notion of Hospitality: Greeks take great pleasure in their hospitality and practice the notion of "filoxenia," which implies offering compassion and generosity to strangers or visitors. Embrace this heritage by participating in polite talks, accepting invitations to neighborhood events, and being open to new experiences. Don't be shocked if locals go out of their way to give help or share their local expertise.

Respect for Historical Sites and Monuments: Greece is home to several historical sites and monuments of significant value, such as the Acropolis and ancient ruins. When visiting these locations, it is necessary to show respect by following the rules and directions presented.

Avoid touching or climbing on the old buildings and be cognizant of the cultural value of these locations.

Dressing Appropriately: Greeks often dress elegantly and take care in their looks. While casual wear is fine in most areas, it is suggested to dress somewhat more formally while visiting churches, monasteries, or other formal businesses. Women may wish to carry a scarf or shawl to cover their shoulders when required.

Traditional Celebrations and traditions: If you have the chance to watch or participate in traditional celebrations and traditions, such as festivals or religious processions, approach them with respect and interest. Observe and follow the example of the locals, and try learning a few simple Greek words to demonstrate your interest and respect.

By adopting Greek customs and traditions, you not only show respect for the local culture but also develop significant ties with the individuals you meet throughout your travels. Remember to approach each meeting with an open mind and a desire to learn, and you'll discover that the Aegean area rewards you with amazing experiences and genuine hospitality.

CHAPTER 10

Planning Your Aegean Adventure: Practical Tips and Resources

Planning an Aegean vacation involves great preparation and study to guarantee a seamless and pleasurable experience. From choosing on the ideal time to come to booking transportation and lodging, here are some practical suggestions and tools to help you organize your Aegean adventure:

Choosing the Right Time to Visit: The Aegean area has a Mediterranean climate, with scorching summers and moderate winters. The peak tourist season normally comes between June and August when the weather is nice and sunny. However, if you want to escape the crowds, try going in the shoulder seasons of spring (April to May) or fall (September to October). During these times, the weather is still good, and you may enjoy a more relaxed environment.

Researching and Selecting Islands: The Aegean is home to a great variety of islands, each with its own particular charm and attractions. Research the various islands to discover which ones correspond with your interests.

Santorini is famed for its breathtaking sunsets and unique blue-domed churches, while Mykonos provides a vibrant nightlife scene. Crete, the biggest Greek island, features a rich history and different scenery. Consider variables such as transportation links, activities, and the environment you seek when picking your island vacations.

Booking Transportation: The Aegean islands are well-connected by numerous transportation alternatives. If you're traveling into Greece, big international airports like Athens International Airport serve as entrances to the Aegean islands.

From Athens, you may access the islands via boat or domestic flights. Research ferry timetables and buy tickets in advance, particularly during the high season, to ensure your chosen travel dates and routes. Several reliable ferry companies operate in the area, such as Blue Star Ferries and Hellenic Seaways.

Housing alternatives: The Aegean islands provide a broad choice of housing alternatives to suit varied tastes and budgets. From luxury resorts to boutique hotels and modest guesthouses, there is something for everyone. Consider lodging in historic villages or near major beaches, depending on your preferences.

Reserving.com and Airbnb are popular portals for locating and reserving lodging, enabling you to browse reviews and compare costs.

Exploring Local food: Greek food is recognized for its fresh ingredients and tasty meals. Embrace the local food scene by sampling classic Greek dishes such as moussaka, souvlaki, and tzatziki.

Explore local tavernas and seafood eateries to enjoy the Aegean's seaside delicacies. Be sure to also taste regional dishes peculiar to each island. Engaging in a food tour or cooking class may give a greater knowledge of Greek cuisine and its cultural importance.

Cultural Etiquette: Familiarize yourself with Greek cultural etiquette and traditions to show respect to the people. Greeks embrace hospitality and appreciate simple gestures such as saying "hello" (kalimera) and "thank you" (efharisto).

Dress modestly while visiting holy locations, and avoid excessive loud or disruptive conduct. Learning a few simple Greek words may help enrich your relationships and demonstrate your interest in the local culture.

Travel Insurance and Health Considerations: It's necessary to have adequate travel insurance to protect oneself in case of unexpected occurrences, such as trip cancellations, medical problems, or lost baggage.

Ensure your insurance covers any adventurous activities you want to pursue, such as hiking or water sports. Additionally, consult with your healthcare professional about any vaccines or health precautions suggested for your travel to Greece.

Local Resources and Guides: Utilize local resources and guides to improve your Aegean vacation. Visit local tourism websites and tourist information offices for up-to-date information on destinations, events, and activities. Engage with local tour providers that offer guided tours and experiences to uncover the hidden jewels and obtain intimate knowledge of the area.

Remember to be flexible in your agenda to allow for unexpected discoveries and leisure time. Embrace the laid-back pace of the Aegean, take in the stunning landscape, and immerse yourself in the rich culture and history of this fascinating area. With careful preparation and an open mind, your Aegean vacation is guaranteed to be a remarkable experience.

Best Time to Visit: Weather and Seasonal Considerations

Determining the ideal time to visit the Aegean area depends on your choices, since each season provides a distinct experience. Understanding the weather patterns and seasonal concerns can help you plan your vacation correctly. Here's an overview of the various seasons and their highlights:

Spring (March to May): Spring is a lovely season to explore the Aegean. The weather begins to warm up, and the surroundings are lush and flowering with bright flowers. It's a wonderful time for outdoor activities like trekking and visiting the historic monuments without the harsh summer heat. The Aegean islands are less congested during this season, providing for a more calm and genuine experience.

Summer (June to August): Summer is the main tourist season in the Aegean, as people come to the islands to soak up the sun and enjoy the colorful environment. The weather is hot and dry, with temperatures reaching their maximum in July and August. The beaches are at their finest, and the Aegean Sea is great for swimming and water sports. Expect congested tourist districts, active nightlife, and a large choice of festivals and events.

Autumn (September to November): Autumn is a great season in the Aegean, with warmer temperatures and less tourists compared to summer. September and October are especially lovely, with warm days and colder nights.

It's an excellent time for touring, since the main places are less crowded. The fall scenery, particularly in the countryside and vineyards, provide a magnificent background for exploring. It's also harvest season, and you may indulge in the fresh fruit and local wines.

Winter (December to February): Winter in the Aegean brings colder temperatures, particularly in the northern regions of the area. The islands receive a warmer winter climate compared to the mainland.

While certain tourist facilities may shut during this season, it's a wonderful time for people wanting a calmer and more personal experience. You may visit the ancient places without the crowds and experience the festive ambiance during Christmas and New Year's festivities.

When arranging your journey, take in mind that the Aegean region includes a broad geographic area, and the weather may differ across islands and coastal locations. It's usually a good idea to examine the precise weather conditions for your desired trip.

In conclusion, the ideal time to visit the Aegean depends on your tastes. Spring and fall bring great weather, less people, and a more relaxed environment. Summer is perfect for beach lovers and people who appreciate exciting nightlife.

Winter gives a unique chance to discover a calmer side of the area and enjoy Christmas events. Consider your interests and preferences, then select the season that matches with your ideal travel experience.

Transportation: Getting Around the Aegean

When traveling the Aegean area, it's crucial to understand the many transportation alternatives available to make the most of your vacation. From island hopping to traveling the mainland, here's a guide to travelling about the Aegean:

Ferries and Catamarans: The Aegean Sea is best experienced by ferry or catamaran, which link the islands and offer a practical and picturesque form of transportation. There are many ferry companies operating in the area, providing a choice of routes and times.

Ferries range in size and amenities, from bigger vessels with restaurants and lounges to smaller boats for shorter excursions. It's advised to check the boat timetables in advance, particularly during the high summer season, and buy your tickets early to guarantee your desired travel dates and times.

Domestic Flights: For larger distances or to access more distant islands, domestic flights are a time-saving choice. Major airports in Athens, Thessaloniki, and other regional hubs provide frequent flights to popular resorts in the Aegean.

The flight length is often brief, and it enables you to cover bigger distances effectively. However, bear in mind that smaller islands may have limited or seasonal flight availability, and it's vital to verify timetables and book in advance.

Rental Cars and Scooters: Renting a car or scooter allows the flexibility to explore at your own leisure, particularly while going on the mainland or bigger islands. Car rental services are accessible at major airports and important tourist locations. Scooters and motorbikes are also popular for short excursions or inside smaller towns and islands. Be careful to educate yourself with local traffic laws and regulations, and always use caution when driving.

Public Transportation: Public transportation, like as buses and trains, is a cheap choice for commuting within the mainland and between major cities. Buses link numerous places, and the network is well-established, dependable, and cost-effective. Trains are provided connecting major cities, delivering a pleasant and picturesque travel. However, it's necessary to verify the timetables in advance, since they may change dependent on the season and location.

Taxis and Ridesharing: Taxis are commonly accessible in large cities and tourist locations. They offer a handy and dependable means of transportation, particularly for shorter distances or when you have baggage. Ensure that the taxi has a functional meter or agree on a fee before commencing the ride. Ridesharing services, such as Uber, are also accessible in some cities and provide an alternative to regular taxis.

Local Transportation: Within towns and cities, local transportation choices such as buses or trams are available for travelling about. They give convenient access to attractions, commercial centers, and local communities. It's important to purchase a transit map or enquire at the local tourist information centers for data on routes, timetables, and costs.

Walking and Cycling: Exploring on foot is a fantastic way to appreciate the charm and beauty of the Aegean. Many cities and islands include pedestrian-friendly streets, small lanes, and seaside promenades that are best explored on foot. Some islands also offer bicycle rentals, enabling you to enjoy gorgeous rides and explore at a leisurely pace.

When organizing your transportation in the Aegean, consider the distances between places, the time of year, and the special demands of your schedule.

Researching and reserving in advance, particularly during the high visitor season, can assist assure smooth and efficient transport throughout your Aegean vacation.

Accommodation and Dining: Choosing the Right Options for Your Trip

Accommodation and eating are vital components of any trip experience, and the Aegean area provides a broad choice of alternatives to suit varied interests and budgets. Here's a guide to help you find the proper hotel and food alternatives for your trip.

Accommodation

Luxury Resorts: Pamper yourself at luxury resorts that provide magnificent vistas, lavish facilities, and world-class service. From infinity pools overlooking the Aegean Sea to private villas with direct beach access, these resorts give a luxurious hideaway.

Recommendations: Amanzoe in Porto Heli, Mystique Santorini in Santorini, and Daios Cove Luxury Resort & Villas in Crete.

Boutique Hotels: Experience customized service and distinct atmospheres at boutique hotels that mix modern design with historic elements.

These smaller-scale lodgings frequently include elegant rooms, cozy surroundings, and dedicated personnel.

Recommendations: Grace Mykonos in Mykonos, Boheme in Santorini, and Casa Delfino Hotel & Spa in Chania.

Traditional Guesthouses: Immerse yourself in local culture by staying in traditional guesthouses. These beautiful lodgings highlight native architecture, genuine hospitality, and a pleasant ambience, allowing for an authentic Aegean experience.

Recommendations: The Windmill Naxos in Naxos, The Three Harites in Paros, and Onar in Andros.

Beachfront Villas: Rent a beachfront villa for a quiet and undisturbed vacation. These large and completely furnished villas enable you to experience the Aegean's splendor from the comfort of your own space, complete with private pools, gardens, and direct access to the beach.

Recommendations: Villa Santorini in Santorini, Villa Pleiades in Mykonos, and Villa Aurora in Rhodes.

Budget-friendly Hotels: For tourists on a budget, there are many of budget-friendly hotels accessible. These motels feature comfortable rooms and basic facilities, making them a reasonable alternative without sacrificing on quality.

Recommendations: Hotel Achilleas in Athens, Hotel Filoxenia in Paros, and Hotel Hermes in Santorini.

Eco-Friendly getaways: Embrace sustainability by vacationing in eco-friendly getaways. These accommodations promote environmental sensitivity, employing renewable energy sources and supporting ethical activities. Enjoy nature-inspired décor, healthy food, and a tranquil location.

Recommendations: Milia Mountain Retreat in Crete, Costa Navarino in Messinia, and Eumelia Organic Agrotourism Farm & Guesthouse in Peloponnese.

Agrotourism lodgings: Experience rural life and agricultural traditions by staying in agrotourism lodgings. These companies frequently provide pleasant accommodations or cottages on working farms, providing you a chance to interact with nature and learn about local agricultural techniques.

Recommendations: To Spitiko tis Kiras Marias in Naxos, Ambelonas Corfu in Corfu, and To Perivoli tis Kyra Katinas in Pelion.

Youth Hostels: For budget-conscious visitors and backpackers, youth hostels give economical housing alternatives. These social centers provide dormitory-style accommodations, community areas, and the possibility to meet other visitors.

Recommendations: Athens Backpackers in Athens, Paraga Beach Hostel in Mykonos, and Santorini Hostel on Santorini.

Vacation Rentals: Renting a vacation house or apartment is a popular alternative for families or parties vacationing together. With fully equipped kitchens and adequate space, vacation rentals give a home-away-from-home feel, enabling you to immerse yourself in local life.

Recommendations: Airbnb and VRBO are wonderful sites to look for holiday properties in the Aegean.

Camping and Glamping: If you appreciate the great outdoors, camping or glamping (luxury camping) is an exciting alternative. Many campsites provide services and amenities, enabling you to connect with nature while enjoying the gorgeous Aegean landscapes.

Recommendations: Apollon Camping in Paros, Camping Drepano in Nafplio, and Gonia Camping in Rhodes.

Dining

Tavernas: Visit traditional tavernas for a real taste of Greek food. These family-run enterprises provide home-style cuisine, emphasizing local tastes and traditions handed down through generations.

Recommendations: To Steki tou Ilia in Athens, O Bakalogatos in Mykonos, and Arismari on Santorini.

Seafood eateries: Given the Aegean's closeness to the sea, seafood eateries abound. Enjoy freshly caught fish, grilled octopus, and other tasty seafood delicacies, typically complemented by gorgeous beach vistas.

Recommendations: Psariston in Athens, Kounelas Fish Tavern on Naxos, and Sunset Fish Tavern in Santorini.

Michelin-Starred Restaurants: For a superb dining experience, indulge in Michelin-starred restaurants that highlight the ingenuity and culinary talent of recognized chefs. These places provide creative meals and great service.

Recommendations: Funky Gourmet in Athens, Matsuhisa Mykonos in Mykonos, and Selene in Santorini.

Local restaurants: Explore local restaurants and street food booths to experience traditional Aegean delicacies at inexpensive costs. Try souvlaki, gyros, spanakopita, and other classic Greek street cuisine specialties.

Recommendations: Souvlaki Grill in Athens, Jimmy's Gyros in Mykonos, and Lucky's Souvlakis in Santorini.

Vineyards: Many vineyards in the Aegean area have its own restaurants, allowing a unique chance to experience local wines coupled with regional food. Enjoy vineyard vistas as you indulge in gastronomic pleasures.

Recommendations: SantoWines in Santorini, Gaia Wines in Nemea, and Porto Carras Winery in Halkidiki.

Farm-to-Table Restaurants: Experience farm-to-table eating at restaurants that value locally produced food. These enterprises promote the freshness and tastes of locally farmed fruit, cheeses, and meats.

Recommendations: Ta Kymata in Paros, Cretan Cuisine in Chania, and Kiki's Tavern in Mykonos.

Rooftop eateries: Take in panoramic views of the Aegean Sea and cityscapes from rooftop eateries. Enjoy a meal or a drink while soaking up the magnificent surroundings and romantic atmospheres.

Recommendations: Galaxy Bar & Restaurant in Athens, 180° Sunset Bar in Mykonos, and Pelican Bay Restaurant in Santorini.

Family-Run Tavernas: Discover hidden treasures by eating at family-run tavernas, where you can experience genuine food and wonderful hospitality. These places frequently provide a comfortable and friendly ambience.

Recommendations: Ta Kardasia in Naxos, Mouria Taverna in Paros, and Mama's House in Mykonos.

Seaside Cafés: Relax in seaside cafés, where you may have a leisurely meal or a refreshing drink with your toes in the sand. These informal places give a laid-back ambiance and a chance to soak up the seaside sensations.

Recommendations: Sirens in Paros, Nikolas Taverna in Mykonos, and Perivolos Beach Bar in Santorini.

Food Festivals: Attend local food festivals to enjoy the Aegean's gastronomic culture at its finest. These events exhibit a broad array of meals, street food, and local delicacies, enabling you to discover and enjoy the region's various tastes.

Recommendations: Food Festival of Naxos, Fisherman's Feast in Paros, and Wine Festival of Santorini.

CONCLUSION

Exploring the Aegean: A Comprehensive Travel Guide to Greece's Timeless Beauty has taken you on a thrilling trip through one of the most stunning locations in the world. From the ancient marvels of Athens to the beautiful islands, from the rich history and mythology to the breathtaking natural vistas, the Aegean has revealed its eternal beauty before your eyes.

Throughout this book, we have studied the cultural richness, historical landmarks, and magnificent landscapes that make the Aegean a must-visit location. We have dug into the ancient ruins and archaeological treasures that bring Greece's past to life, uncovering the legends of gods and heroes. We have basked in the sun-kissed magnificence of its beaches, sailed across its crystal-clear seas, and trekked its mountainous trails, immersing ourselves in the region's natural beauties.

We have loved the tastes of traditional Greek cuisine, from the exquisite fish and olive oil to the tangy feta cheese and local delicacies. We have rejoiced with locals at vivid festivals, danced to traditional music, and experienced the cultural rituals and traditions that define the Aegean's uniqueness.

Practical information, advice, and recommendations have led you through every part of your trip, creating a flawless and wonderful experience. From picking the ideal islands for your schedule to locating the best lodgings and eating alternatives, we have equipped you with the tools to organize a vacation that meets your interests and budget.

As you begin on your Aegean trip, may this handbook be your trusty friend, bringing insights and inspiration along the way. Whether you're a history aficionado, a nature lover, a gastronomic adventurer, or a seeker of real cultural experiences, the Aegean has something to offer everyone.

As you step foot on these ancient lands, immerse yourself in the timeless splendor that surrounds you. Let the legends of the past merge with the dynamic present, and let the Aegean's charm capture your senses. From the busy streets of Athens to the peaceful coastlines of the islands, let Greece's timeless beauty leave an everlasting impact on your heart and spirit.

Bon voyage, and may your trip across the Aegean be full with exploration, amazement, and amazing experiences.

Printed in Great Britain
by Amazon

23970251R00089